DR. BILAL PHILIPS'

THE TRUE MESSAGE OF

JESUS CHRIST

A REPLY, REFUTATION AND REBUTTAL

BY

A. YOUSEF AL-KATIB

TIME 🏛 BOOKS

Dr. Bilal Philips'
The True Message of Jesus Christ:
A Reply, Refutation and Rebuttal

ISBN (13) (Paperback): 978-1-68109-090-0
ISBN (10) (Paperback): 1-68109-090-2
ISBN (13) (eBook): 978-1-68109-091-7
ISBN (10) (eBook): 1-68109-091-0

Time Books™
an imprint of TellerBooks™
TellerBooks.com/Time_Books

t TellerBooks

www.TellerBooks.com

Manufactured in the U.S.A.

NOTE: Unless otherwise stated herein, all biblical Scriptures quoted herein are taken from the New King James Version or American Standard Version translations, unless the verses are quoted directly from Dr. Philips's book, in which case other translations may be used.

DISCLAIMER: The opinions, views, positions and conclusions expressed in this volume reflect those of the individual author and not necessarily those of the publisher or any of its imprints, editors or employees.

About the Imprint

The *Reply, Refutation and Rebuttal* Series™ of Time Books™ publishes monographs and treatises that reply to contemporary perspectives on political, philosophical and religious issues.

Complete your collection with the following titles:

- Dinesh D'Souza's *What's So Great About America*: A Reply, Refutation and Rebuttal
- Dr. Greg Boyd's *Myth of a Christian Nation*: A Reply, Refutation and Rebuttal
- Dr. Mel White's *What the Bible Says and Doesn't Say About Homosexuality*: A Reply, Refutation and Rebuttal
- Dr. H. M. Baagil's *Muslim-Christian Dialogue*: A Reply, Refutation and Rebuttal
- Karl Marx and Friedrich Engels' *The Communist Manifesto*: A Reply, Refutation and Rebuttal
- Fouad Masri's *Is the Injeel Corrupted?* A Reply, Refutation and Rebuttal
- Dr. Bilal Philips' *The True Message of Jesus Christ*: A Reply, Refutation and Rebuttal

TIME 🏛 BOOKS

The mission of Time Books™ is to reintroduce time-tested values and truths to modern debates on political, economic, and moral issues. The imprint focuses on books and monographs dealing with society, ethics, and public policy.

Contents

Abbreviations

English Translations of the Bible:

ASV .... American Standard Version
BBE .... Bible in Basic English
Darby .... Darby Bible
ESV .... English Standard Version
ISV .... International Standard Version
KJV .... King James Version
MKJV .... Modern King James Version
NIV .... New International Version
NKJV .... New King James Version
RSV .... Revised Standard Version

Books of the Bible:

1Ch .... 1 Chronicles
1Co .... 1 Corinthians
1Jn .... 1 John
1Ki .... 1 Kings
1Pe .... 1 Peter
1Sa .... 1 Samuel
1Th .... 1 Thessalonians
1Ti .... 1 Timothy
2Ch .... 2 Chronicles
2Co .... 2 Corinthians
2Jn .... 2 John
2Ki .... 2 Kings
2Pe .... 2 Peter
2Sa .... 2 Samuel
2Th .... 2 Thessalonians
2Ti .... 2 Timothy
3Jo .... 3 John
Acts .... Book of Acts
Amos .... Book of Amos
Col .... Colossians
Dan .... Daniel
Deu .... Deuteronomy
Ecc .... Ecclesiastes
Eph .... Ephesians

Est ....Esther
Exo ....Exodus
Eze................Ezekiel
Ezr ....Book of Ezra
Gal................Galatians
Gen................Genesis
Hab................Habakkuk
Hag................Haggai
Heb................Hebrews
Hos ....Hosea
Isa ....Isaiah
Jas................James
Jer ....Jeremiah
Job ....Book of Job
Joel ....Book of Joel
John ....Gospel of John
Jon ....Jonah
Jos ....Joshua
Jude ....Book of Jude
Jdg ....Judges
Lam ....Lamentations
Lev ....Leviticus
Luke ....Gospel of Luke
Mal ....Malachi
Mark.,,,,.... .....Gospel of Mark
Mat ....Gospel of Matthew
Mic ....Micah
Nah................Nahum
Neh................Nehemiah
Num................Numbers
Oba................Obadiah
Phm ....Philemon
Php ....Philippians
Pro................Proverbs
Psa................Psalms
Rev ....Revelation
Rom................Romans
Ruth................Book of Ruth
Son ....Song of Solomon

Chapter 1. Introduction

In *The True Message of Jesus Christ*, Dr. Bilal Philips claims that Jesus Christ was merely a prophet of *Allāh* who reaffirmed the central message that was later revealed to Muhammad. Dr. Philips argues that although Jesus claimed to be the Son of God in the Bible, modern translations of the Bible are corruptions of the original revelations given by *Allāh*. Only the *Qur'ān*, which downgrades Jesus' status from the Son of God to a prophet, reflects God's true, uncorrupted message.

This *Reply* to *The True Message of Jesus Christ* demonstrates that Dr. Philips' arguments are flawed and suffer from serious weaknesses on multiple levels. First, Dr. Philips' claims are not historically grounded. Second, he misconstrues the text and meanings of the Bible. Third, he employs circular reasoning to support his assertions. Fourth, the claims Dr. Philips makes with respect to the corruption of the Bible conflict with even the teachings of the *Qur'ān* on the divine inspiration of the Torah and other Hebrew and Christian scriptures.

Some of Dr. Philips' claims about the Bible are correct, though ultimately, they relate to minor or ancillary points, such as discrepancies in extant biblical manuscripts as to a king's age when he began to rule. While such minor discrepancies exist, they should be expected in the copying and transmission of texts over thousands of years and they do not suggest deliberate falsification of the text for dogmatic purposes. Such discrepancies do not alter the overall message of the Bible—that "God so loved the world that he gave His one and only Son, so that everyone who believes in him will have eternal life" (John 3:16).

The True Message of Jesus Christ fails to persuasively demonstrate that man has corrupted the Bible, that the *Qur'ān* is God's true and divinely inspired book and that Jesus' true message is that He is merely a prophet of *Allāh*, rather than God's sacrificial lamb, offered "as the atoning sacrifice for our sins, and not only for ours but also for the sins of the whole world" (1 John 2:2). Ultimately, the book fails to defeat the hope given to all who put their faith and trust in Jesus Christ.

Chapter 2. Use of Sources to Challenge Christianity

A. Overview

Dr. Philips' first flaw is the way in which he uses sources to cast doubt on the reliability of the Bible. He combs through the literature of Western scholars and even some Christian clerics, searching for any arguments he can find that question Jesus's historicity or the divine inspiration of the Bible. He then reproduces these arguments without any original commentary or logical flow.

B. Problems with Dr. Philips' Approach

There are several problems with his approach:

1. Sources that Cannot Be Found

The sources, for the most part, cannot be found. He cites, for example, magazine articles published decades ago, which cannot be found anywhere on the Internet or accessed to study the full context of the statements quoted and the claims made or to even verify whether Dr. Philips is quoting them correctly. He frequently cites articles published by major magazines and newspapers such as *Time* magazine and *The Times*, London, which if they existed would normally be found with relative ease, since these publications have online archives. *The Times*, for example, has an archive going back to the Nineteenth Century! Yet Internet searches on Google only turn up Islamic proselytization websites and Islamic tracts rather than the original sources. Therefore, the reader is unable to verify that Dr. Philips is accurately quoting from the original sources and to obtain the full context of the material being quoted. Examples of articles that he quotes that cannot be found or verified online are as follows:

- Dr. J.K. Elliott's article published in *The Times*, London (10th Sept., 1987) entitled "Checking the Bible's Roots" (quoted on p. 10).

2. Dr. Philips Only Proves that There Are Scholars Who Challenge the Reliability of the Bible

Even if the sources are properly being quoted and used within the proper context, the use of these sources at most only proves that there is a group of scholars and clerics who do not ascribe to the divine authority of the Scriptures. One need not enter into a prolonged study or publish a book to prove this point; it is common knowledge that there have been learned atheists and scholars who have rejected Christianity and the Bible since the very origins of Christianity. In his classic work, *Confessions*, St. Augustine goes to great length in explaining how he was one of these "learned scholars" before he encountered God at Ostia and surrendered to Jesus.

Dr. Philips has done no service to the debate over the truth of Christianity by combing through some obscure sources, finding some scholars who argue that the Christian Scriptures are not reliable and then quoting them verbatim in his book. He would have done a better service to the debate had he actually developed arguments in his favor or attempted to show contradictions in the Scriptures or other indicia of unreliability rather than merely reproduce the conclusions of other scholars without giving the reader the chance to review, challenge or engage these other scholars.

In the West, where democracy protects free inquiry and freedom of religion, thought and expression, it comes without surprise that not everyone believes in the divine inspiration of the Scriptures. Yet the use of these sources in attempting to prove the unreliability of the Christian Scriptures is no more useful than a compilation of scholarly sources challenging the divine inspiration of the *Qur'ān* as evidence of the unreliability of the *Qur'ān*. Without actually engaging the underlying evidence treated in the sources, the compilation serves nothing more than proving that there are some scholars who doubt the divine inspiration of the *Qur'ān*, a point that need not be proven.

Chapter 3. Individual Claims and Replies

A. The Authors of the Gospels Are Unknown

1. Matthew

a) *Matthew as Anonymous*

(1) Argument

Dr. Philip writes (p. 20):

> Although Matthew, Luke and John are the names of disciples of Jesus, the authors of the Gospels bearing their names were not those famous disciples, but other individuals who used the disciples' names to give their accounts credibility. In fact, all the Gospels originally circulated anonymously. Authoritative names were later assigned to them by unknown figures in the early church.30

He issues the following reference to support his claim with respect to the Book of Matthew:

> "Although there is a Matthew named among the various lists of Jesus' disciples...the writer of Matthew is probably anonymous." The New Encyclopaedia Britannica, vol. 14, p. 826.

(2) Response

(a) The Encyclopedia Britannica Argument is Invalid

Dr. Philips failed to include the entire excerpt, which states[1]:

> Although there is a Matthew named among the various lists of Jesus' disciples, more telling is the fact that the name of Levi, the

---

[1] See https://www.britannica.com/topic/biblical-literature/The-Synoptic-Gospels.

tax collector who in Mark became a follower of Jesus, in Matthew is changed to Matthew. It would appear from this that Matthew was claiming apostolic authority for his Gospel through this device but that the writer of Matthew is probably anonymous.

There are several problems with Dr. Philips' argument:

- He cites Encyclopedia Britannica, which is not a definitive or authoritative source on religious doctrine;
- The source he cites does not definitively state whether the author of Matthew was the apostle Matthew; it simply states that the writer is "probably anonymous."
- If Matthew was in fact "claiming apostolic authority for his Gospel through this device" (i.e., the device of authoring the book "Matthew"), then this would further give support to the theory that it was Matthew the apostle rather than another third party that authored the book.
- The Encyclopedia Britannica article, based on the fact that Levi's name, meaning to "take," is changed to "Matthew," meaning "gift of the Lord" in Hebrew, concludes that a book in the Bible named "Matthew" could not have possibly been written by the apostle Matthew because the word "Matthew" is used as a title rather than as a personal name. Such an argument does not hold water; Matthew was an actual name used in biblical Judea. The fact that one man's name was changed to Matthew cannot be used as a basis to conclude that the name was a mere title that others, including the author of the Gospel of Matthew, could not have validly held and been identified by.

(b) Matthew's Use of Texts from Mark

Some critics dispute the Apostle Matthew's authorship of the Gospel on the basis of the Gospel's apparent reliance on Mark's account. However, reliance on another account does not undermine Matthew's authorship. An eyewitness can reaffirm the accounts told by another witness or even a non-witness without undermining his or her own testimony of the accounts in question. The NIV Study Bible summarizes expresses this point clearly (p. 1439):

> The early church fathers were unanimous in holding that Matthew, one of the 12 apostles, was the author of this Gospel. However, the results of modern critical studies—in particular those that stress

Matthew's alleged dependence on Mark for a substantial party of his Gospel—have caused some Biblical scholars to abandon Matthean authorship. Why, they ask, would Matthew, an eyewitness to the events of our Lord's life, depend so heavily on Mark's account? The best answer seems to be that he agreed with it and wanted to show that the apostolic testimony to Christ was not divided.

b) Rejection of the View that the Apostle Matthew wrote the Gospel of Matthew

(1) Argument

Dr. Philips writes (p. 21-22):

> J.B. Phillips, a prebendary of the Chichester Cathedral, the Anglican Church of England, wrote the following preface for his translation of the Gospel according to St. Matthew: "Early tradition ascribed this Gospel to the apostle Matthew, but scholars nowadays almost all reject this view. The author, whom we can conveniently call Matthew, has plainly drawn on the mysterious "Q", which may have been a collection of oral traditions. He has used Mark's Gospel freely, though he has rearranged the order of events and has in several instances used different words for what is plainly the same story."

(2) Response

Matthew's drawing on third sources, including the mysterious "Q" and the Gospel of Mark, does not undermine the eyewitness testimony of that author. It is possible that the author drew on third party sources to corroborate his own testimony or to supplement it if he was not in a particular place in a particular time. For example, church tradition holds that Matthew only became an eyewitness of Jesus's life after he was called by Jesus. Therefore, he could not have been an eyewitness to all of the events that precede his calling. This includes, but is not limited to, the following:

-   Jesus's genealogy, written of in Matthew 1;
-   The birth of Jesus, written of in Matthew 2;
-   The narrative of John the Baptist, in Matthew 3;
-   The temptation of Jesus, in Matthew 4.

In fact, Matthew 9 is the first time we hear of Matthew the tax collector (Levi) in the Gospel of Matthew. The fact that Matthew used other sources for earlier chapters of his Gospel or even as supplements for later chapters does not preclude the possibility that the Gospel was written by an Apostle. The Apostle Matthew could not have been in all places at all times; it would not be unusual for him to rely on other sources to complete his Gospel.

2. Mark

a) Argument

Dr. Philips writes (p. 19):

> The New Testament Gospel of Mark, though considered by Church scholars to be the oldest of the Gospels, was not written by a disciple of Jesus. Biblical scholars concluded, based on the evidence contained in the Gospel, that Mark himself was not a disciple of Jesus. Furthermore, according to them, it is not even certain who Mark really was. The ancient Christian author, Eusebius (325 C.E.), reported that another ancient author, Papias (130 C.E.), was the first to attribute the Gospel to John Mark, a companion of Paul.29 Others suggested that he may have been the scribe of Peter and yet others hold that he was probably someone else.

Dr. Philips further cites The Encyclopedia Britannica to argue that the writer of the Gospel of Mark is unknown. He writes (p. 20):

> "Though the author of Mark is probably unknown..." *The New Encyclopaedia Britannica*, vol. 14, p. 824.

b) Response

(1) Who Was Mark?

(a) Tradition

Tradition holds that this book was written by John Mark, who accompanied Paul and Barnabas on their missionary journeys, and caused Paul and Barnabas's split based on Paul's view that John Mark was unreliable.

(b) The Companion of Paul and Barnabas

According to the Zondervan *NIV Study Bible*, there is no direct internal evidence of authorship, but it was the unanimous testimony of the early church that the Gospel of Mark was written by John Mark ("John, also called Mark," Acts 12:12, 25; 15:37), an assistant accompanying Paul and Barnabas on their missionary journeys and whom Paul did not want to bring with them because John Mark had withdrawn in Pamphylia:

> Acts 13:5 And when they arrived in Salamis, they preached the word of God in the synagogues of the Jews. They also had John as their assistant.
>
> …
>
> Acts 13:13 Now when Paul and his party set sail from Paphos, they came to Perga in Pamphylia; and John, departing from them, returned to Jerusalem.
>
> …
>
> Acts 15:36 Then after some days Paul said to Barnabas, "Let us now go back and visit our brethren in every city where we have preached the word of the Lord, and see how they are doing."
>
> Acts 15:37 Now Barnabas was determined to take with them John called Mark.
>
> Acts 15:38 But Paul insisted that they should not take with them the one who had departed from them in Pamphylia, and had not gone with them to the work.
>
> Acts 15:39 Then the contention became so sharp that they parted from one another. And so Barnabas took Mark and sailed to Cyprus;
>
> Acts 15:40 but Paul chose Silas and departed, being commended by the brethren to the grace of God.
>
> Acts 15:41 And he went through Syria and Cilicia, strengthening the churches.

(c) The Disciple Who Fled Naked in the Garden

John Mark, the companion of Paul and Barnabas noted above, is also viewed by Church tradition to be the "young man" noted in Mark 14:51, who followed Jesus after his arrest.

> Mark 14:51 Now a certain young man followed Him, having a linen cloth thrown around his naked body. And the young men laid hold of him,
>
> Mark 14:52 and he left the linen cloth and fled from them naked.

The notes of *The NIV Study Bible* state (p. 1526):

> *A young man.* Not specifically identified, but this anonymity may suggest that this was John Mark, writer of this Gospel. *a linen garment.* Ordinarily the outer garment was made of wool. The fine linen garment left behind in the hand of a guard indicates that the youth was from a wealthy family.

If the "young man" in Mark 14 is in fact the author of the Book of Mark, then Mark would have been an <u>eyewitness</u>.

(d) Papias's Account of John Mark

According to *The NIV Study Bible*, the most important evidence of John Mark's authorship comes from Papias (c. 140 AD), who quotes an earlier source as saying:

-   John Mark was a close associate of Peter, from whom he received the tradition of the things said and done by the Lord;
-   This tradition did not come to John Mark as a finished, sequential account of the life of our Lord, but as the preaching of Peter— preaching directed to the needs of the early Christian communities;
-   Mark accurately preserved this material.

(e) Mark as Peter's Scribe

The conclusion drawn from this tradition is that the Gospel of Mark largely consists of the preaching of Peter arranged and shaped by Mark. According to this tradition, Mark was a disciple of Peter and so an "apostolic man" who received from Peter's preaching the tradition of the things said and done by Jesus.

(2) Modern Scholarship

It is true that some modern scholars doubt the Markan tradition and regard the author as unknown. Delbert Burkett, *An introduction to the New Testament and the origins of Christianity*, Cambridge University Press (2002), p. 156.

With respect to the Encyclopedia Britannica citation, Dr. Philips again does not reference the entire citation, which states[2]:

> Though the author of Mark is probably unknown, authority is traditionally derived from a supposed connection with the Apostle Peter, who had transmitted the traditions before his martyr death under Nero's persecution (c. 64–65). Papias, a 2nd-century bishop in Asia Minor, is quoted as saying that Mark had been Peter's amanuensis (secretary) who wrote as he remembered (after Peter's death), though not in the right order. Because Papias was from the East, perhaps the Johannine order would have priority, as is the case in the structure of the Syrian scholar Tatian's Diatesseron (harmony of the Gospels).

> Attempts have been made to identify Mark as the John Mark mentioned in Acts 12 or as the disciple who fled naked in the garden (Mark 14). A reference to "my son, Mark," in I Peter is part of the same tradition by which Mark was related to Peter; thus the Evangelist's apostolic guarantor was Peter.

(3) Observations

If we trust church tradition, then we can conclude that the author of the Gospel of Mark was Peter's disciple John Mark. If it was, then the Gospel of Mark was written by a close associate of Peter, from whom he received the tradition of the things said and done by the Lord. If, in addition to this, the author of the Gospel of Mark is the "young man" referenced in Mark 14:51-52, then the author would have also been an eyewitness.

Critical legal studies have not proffered any compelling reason to doubt John Mark's authorship of the Gospel of Mark.

3. Luke

a) Argument

Dr. Philips argues that the author of the Gospel of Luke is "unknown" (p. 20). He cites the Encyclopedia Britannica, which states:

---

[2]   Available   at   <https://www.britannica.com/topic/biblical-literature/The-Synoptic-Gospels>.

The Muratorian Canon refers to Luke, the physician, Paul's companion; Irenaeus depicts Luke as a follower of Paul's gospel. Eusebius has Luke as an Antiochene physician who was with Paul in order to give the Gospel apostolic authority." *The New Encyclopaedia Britannica*, vol. 14, p. 827.

b) Response

It is ironic and contradictory that Dr. Philips would, on the one hand, write that the author of the Gospel of Luke is "unknown," while at the same time cite as his source an Encyclopedia Britannica entry that in turn cites various sources that identify Luke as:

- A physician, Paul's companion;
- A follower of Paul's gospel;
- An Antiochian physician who was with Paul in order to give the Gospel apostolic authority

All of these accounts are consistent with one another and reaffirm that Luke was both a doctor and disciple of Paul.

4. John

a) Argument

Dr. Philips writes (p. 22):

The Fourth Gospel (John) was opposed as heretical in the early church, and it knows none of the stories associated with John, son of Zebedee. In the judgement of many scholars, it was produced by a "school" of disciples, probably in Syria in the last decade of the first century.

b) Response

(1) Overview

Dr. Philips' main flaw here is that he simply cites another source, *The Five Gospels*, that argues that the Gospel of John was not written by John the Apostle. He offers no evidence to back up his view. If finding some author who has written that a particular fact is nor is not true is an indication that it is or is not true, then it would not be difficult to disprove the whole of Islam by simply citing some study whereby one scholar found the claims of the religion to be false. To engage in true academic scholarship and debate, one must be ready to present evidence and make arguments, not merely state that someone else found something to be true. For every source that Dr. Philips can cite to argue that the Gospel of John was not written by the Apostle John, it is possible to find ten more than argue that it was written. To get past this, it is necessary to examine the actual evidence backing up each respective argument.

(2) Arguments in Favor of the Apostle John's Authorship

The Gospel of John is held by tradition to be written by John, one of the Twelve Apostles. John the Apostle was the son of Zebedee and the younger brother of James, son of Zebedee. According to Church tradition, their mother was Salome.

Zebedee, James and John were fisherman in the Sea of Galilee. Matthew recounts that after Jesus called Simon and Peter, who were also fishermen, He "saw two other brothers, James the son of Zebedee, and John his brother, in the boat with Zebedee their father, mending their nets. He called them, and immediately they left the boat and their father, and followed Him" (Mat 4:21-22). According to church tradition, John was therefore an <u>eyewitness</u>.

The Gospel of John has indications that suggest it was based on the recollections of an eyewitness. He recounts, for example, that the house at Bethany was filled with the fragrance of the broken perfume jar (John 12:30).

Moreover, early church fathers such as Irenaeus and Tertullian universally held that John wrote this Gospel.

B. Jesus's Historicity Challenged

1. Claim

Dr. Philips writes (p. 7-8):

> A biblical scholar, R.T. France, writes, "No 1st century inscription mentions him and no object or building has survived which has a specific link to him." This fact has even led some Western historians to mistakenly claim that Jesus Christ never actually existed. Therefore, research has to be primarily based on the scriptures which address the person and the mission of Jesus Christ. The scriptures in question are those officially recognized by both Christianity and Islam.

2. Response

Dr. Philips' claim is flawed for two reasons:

-   It is wholly inaccurate to state that "No 1st century inscription mentions [Jesus] and no object or building has survived which has a specific link to him." R. T. France's prestigious academic reputation aside, it is unclear whether R. T. France ever stated this, as we were unable to access the source (*Time*, December 18, 1995, p. 46.). Even if he did, however, state it, it would be patently wrong, as the Gospel manuscripts are first century "objects" that all present the life of Jesus and thus have a "specific link" to him:

    o   The Gospel of Matthew is dated 40 – 115 AD;
    o   The Gospel of Mark is dated 55 to 70 AD;
    o   The Gospel of Luke is dated around 60 AD;
    o   The Gospel of John is dated around 80 – 90 AD.

-   Dr. Philips further writes that "research has to be primarily based on the scriptures which address the person and the mission of Jesus Christ. The scriptures in question are those officially recognized by both Christianity and Islam." His statement is, however, misleading in that it implies the existence of a common corpus of Scriptures referencing Jesus that are recognized by both Christianity and Islam, but this is not the case; the Christian Scriptures recognizing Jesus are deemed by Islam to be corruptions of the true, original manuscripts, and Christians do not consider the *Qur'ān* to be the inspired word of God.

C. The Books of the Bible Cannot be Accorded Verbal Divine Authority

1. Claim: Western Christianity Has Accepted that the Bible Cannot be Accorded Divine Authority

Dr. Philips quotes from the preface of *The Myth of God Incarnate*, where the editor writes (p. 8):

> In the nineteenth century, Western Christianity … accepted that the books of the Bible were written by a variety of human beings in a variety of circumstances, and cannot be accorded a verbal divine authority.

2. Response: The Groups Referenced Represent Fringe Rather Than
    Orthodox Christianity

This claim is problematic for several reasons. While certainly there
may be individual Christians or groups that as early as the nineteenth
century rejected the notion that the books of the Bible can be accorded
with divine authority, by and large, these individuals or groups represent
the fringe of Christianity, falling far out of Orthodox Christian circles.
Today, orthodox Christianity, whether it takes the form of the Orthodox
Church, the Catholic Church or the Evangelical Protestant churches,
maintain the divine inspiration of the Bible. There are some scholars and
members of certain denominations (predominantly many of the liturgical
Protestant denominations) that reject the divine inspiration of the Bible,
but this can be no more evidence of the unreliability of the Bible than
can individual Muslims who question the divine inspiration of the
Qur'ān serve as evidence of the lack of historical reliability of the
Qur'ān. There are many diverse views in every religious group.

D. Contradictions in the Bible

1. Whether God or Satan Provoked David to Number Israel

a) Claim

Dr. Philips writes (p. 23):

> The authors of Samuel and Chronicles relate the same story about
> Prophet David taking a census of the Jews. However, in 2nd
> Samuel, it states that Prophet David acted on God's instructions,
> while in 1st Chronicles, he acted on Satan's instructions.

Dr. Philips quotes the following passages:

-   2Sa 24:1 Again the anger of the <u>Lord</u> was aroused against Israel,
    and <u>He moved David</u> against them to say, "Go, number Israel and
    Judah."
-   1Ch 21:1 Now <u>Satan stood up against Israel</u>, and moved David to
    number Israel.

b) Response

The apparent contradiction can be reconciled by viewing it as a
difference in emphasis between the author of 2 Samuel and the author of
1 Chronicles. Satan directly moved David to number Israel, but as with

all acts, he was only able to move with God's permission. Therefore, while Satan was the active agent and direct cause, God acted as a principal with indirect control over David's act.

Therefore, Satan provoked David directly (1 Chronicles 21:1), but God gave Satan permission to do so, as we see in the book of Job. In Job, Satan presents himself before the Lord and requests God's permission to afflict his faithful servant, Job. The devil insists that Job only serves God because of His blessings, and he would surely curse God if he were tested. God conditionally grants Satan's request.

We should also consider the emphases of the respective authors of 2 Samuel (probably Nathan or Gad), who viewed the affair in the sense of God's ultimate control over all things, and the author of 1 Chronicles (probably Ezra), who emphasized the satanic plot and how God used this as a tool for judgment. That 2 Samuel focuses on God as the mover finds support in the fact that Nathan and Gad were prophets who proclaimed God's control over the affairs of men. Ezra, in contrast, was a priest interested in pointing out the holiness of God and who hates sin.

2. The Plague Prophesied by Gad: Three Years or Seven Years

a) Claim

Dr. Philips writes (p. 21):

> In describing the length of a plague prophesied by Gad, the author of 2nd Samuel listed it as seven years, while the author of 1st Chronicles listed it as three years.

II SAMUEL 24:13

So Gad came to David and told him, and said unto him, "Shall <u>seven years</u> of famine come unto thee in thy land? or wilt thou flee three months before thine enemies, while they pursue thee?"

I CHRONICLES 21:11

11 So Gad came to David, and said unto him, "Thus saith the Lord, 'Choose thee 12 Either <u>three years' famine</u>; or three months to be destroyed before thy foes, while that the sword of thine enemies overtaketh thee;' "

b) Response

(1) Explanation 1: 2 Samuel Adds Four Years of Initial Famine to the Three Additional Years Offered

(a) Overview

Several web sites, including "7 years or 3 years of famine?"[3] give the following explanation:

> In reality, Gad offered David 3 years of famine in addition to the 4 that had already transpired by that point. 2 Samuel gives an account of the 4 years that had already transpired and the 3 additional years for a total of 7 years, which are offered to David; 1 Chronicles gives the account of *only* the 3 additional years of famine.
>
> In 2Sa 21:1, we read: "Now there was a famine in the days of David for three years, year after year."
>
> Thereafter, in 2Sa 24:8, we read, "So when they had gone through all the land, they came to Jerusalem at the end of nine months and twenty days."
>
> The only way to reconcile this apparent contradiction, as well as that recorded in the Exodus 20 and Deuteronomy 5 accounts, is to recognize that the quotation marks we find in many modern translations do not exist in the original texts (both the Hebrew Old Testament and Greek New Testament do not include quotation marks).[4] This is because the biblical writers did not intend to give exact quotes of each word spoken. The insertion of quotation marks in modern translations give the false idea that authors quoted word-for-word, which is not the case. When reading the Scriptures, we should recognize the *ideas* that are poured forward. Although their exact word-for-word presentation may vary, the ideas put forward by different accounts of the same event are always consistent with one another.

(b) Potential Issue with this Explanation

3

http://blessedquietness.com/journal/housechu/three_years_or_seven_years_of_famine.htm.

[4] The King James Version of the Bible, recognizing this truth, does not insert quotes in its translation..

The only potential issue with this explanation is that it assumes, without any apparent evidence, that the famine continued in the period between:

-   The first three years of famine; and
-   God's offer to David of new famine of three years (for a total of seven).

In other words, a famine continued during the following periods:

-   The three years of famine;
-   During the killing of the Philistines (2Sa 23:12), which would have had to have taken two months and ten days;
-   The nine months and twenty days for taking the census (2Sa 24:8).

This would have equaled a total of four years, which, when added to the additional three years referenced in 1 Chronicles, would come out to a total of seven years.

However, we do not know whether the famine continued during the killing of the Philistines in 2 Samuel 23:12 or in the nine months and twenty days for taking the census in 2 Samuel 24:8.

(2) Explanation 2: Translators' Error

The Treasury of Scriptural Knowledge provides the following commentary on 1 Chronicles 21:12:

> three years' famine: In 2Sa_24:13, it is <u>seven years</u>; but the [Greek] Septuagint has there τρια ετη [Strong's G5140], three years, as here; which is, no doubt, the true reading; the letter ז, zayin, seven, being mistaken for ג, gimmel, three. Lev_26:26-29; 2Sa_21:1, 2Sa_24:13; 1Ki_17:1; 2Ki_8:1; Lam_4:9; Luk_4:25

If we accept this explanation, we can conclude that the KJV and several other English translations of the Bible mistook the Hebrew ג, gimmel, three for the letter ז, zayin, seven when preparing their translations. In other words, the translators of the Bible into English were not infallible.

(3) Conclusion

According to the explanations proposed above, we can conclude that one of the following is true:

- The authors of the KJV and other translations of the Bible that use seven years in 2 Samuel 24:13 mistook the Hebrew ג, gimmel, three for the letter ז, zayin, seven; or
- The author of the original Hebrew manuscript of 2 Samuel 24:13 did in fact use the Hebrew letter ז, zayin, seven, but in so doing, he was counting the three years of initial famine recounted in 2 Samuel 21:1 plus the 9 months and 20 days for taking the census in 2 Samuel 24:8.

Neither of these explanations poses a grave problem or threat to the integrity of the Bible. Mistaking a number is an innocent error with no grave consequences that does not cast into question the overall message of the Bible; if anything, it simply reinforces the biblical teaching that man is imperfect and that only God is infallible; the translators of the Bible, like all men, are fallible. That they might make a mistake in translating the text does not cast into doubt the validity of the original text.

The alternate explanation simply shows that different books of the Bible propose using different counting methodologies, with one book (2 Samuel) choosing to aggregate the total number of years of famine and the second book (1 Chronicles) choosing instead to highlight only the additional time (3 years) being aggregated to the past famine.

3. The Number of Syrians Who Died in Battle

a) Overview

Dr. Philips writes (p. 22):

> The author of 2nd Samuel described the number of Syrians who died during a battle with Prophet David as being seven hundred, while the author of 1st Chronicles gave their number as seven thousand.

b) Comparison of Translations

	2 Samuel 10:18	1 Chronicles 19:18
NIV	David killed *seven hundred of their charioteers* and forty thousand of their foot soldiers.	David killed *seven thousand of their charioteers* and forty thousand of their foot soldiers.

NKJV	David killed *seven hundred charioteers* and forty thousand horsemen of the Syrians	David killed *seven thousand charioteers* and forty thousand foot soldiers of the Syrians
KJV	And the Syrians fled before Israel; and David slew *the men of seven hundred chariots* of the Syrians, and forty thousand horsemen	David slew of the Syrians *seven thousand men which fought in* **chariots**, and forty thousand footmen
KJV+	And the Syrians[H758] fled[H5127] before[H4480 H6440] Israel;[H3478] and David[H1732] slew[H2026] *the men of* seven[H7651] hundred[H3967] chariots[H7393] of the Syrians,[H4480 H758] and forty[H705] thousand[H505] horsemen[H6571]	David[H1732] slew[H2026] of the Syrians[H4480 H758] seven[H7651] thousand[H505] *men which fought in* chariots,[H7393] and forty[H705] thousand[H505] footmen,[H376 H7273]

c) Possible Explanation 1: There is a Genuine Error

Various commentaries conclude that there is a genuine error due to the way numerals were expressed with letters in the Hebrew. The NIV Study Bible note at 2 Samuel 10:18 states:

> Evidently a copyist's mistake; in 1Ch 19:18 the figure is 7,000.

Albert Barnes' *Notes on the Bible* states:

> Seven hundred chariots - More probable than the "seven thousand" of 1Ch_19:18. The frequent errors in numbers arise from the practice of expressing numerals by letters, with one or more dots or dashes to indicate hundreds, thousands, etc.

Adam Clarke's *Commentary on the Bible* states:

> In the parallel place, 1Ch_19:18, it is said, David slew of the Syrians Seven Thousand men, which fought in chariots. It is difficult to ascertain the right number in this and similar places. It is very probable that, in former times, the Jews expressed, as they often do now, their numbers, not by words at full length, but by numeral letters; and, as many of the letters bear a great similarity to each

other, mistakes might easily creep in when the numeral letters came to be expressed by words at full length. This alone will account for the many mistakes which we find in the numbers in these books, and renders a mistake here very probable. The letter ז zain, with a dot above, stands for seven thousand, נ nun for seven hundred: the great similarity of these letters might easily cause the one to be mistaken for the other, and so produce an error in this place.

That there is a genuine error is one possible explanation of the evident contradiction, though other explanations are possible.

d) Possible Explanation 2: 7,000 Men in 700 Chariots Were Slain

(1) Overview

Some argue that David slew 7,000 men in 700 chariots.

This is the approach of the KJV, which translates 2 Samuel 10:18 as follows:

> David slew *the men of* seven hundred chariots of the Syrians, and forty thousand *horsemen*, and smote Shobach the captain of their host, who died there.

(2) Problem with Explanation

The words "the men of," which are found in the KJV in a gray italic font, are "supplied words" that the translators added for clarity in the English language, but that are lacking in the original Hebrew. The lack of Strong's numbers behind them is an indicator that there is not a specific Hebrew or Greek word behind them. The addition of "the men of" is thus potentially problematic as it is not found in the original Hebrew manuscripts. Rather, the original Hebrew states as follows:

- 2 Samuel 10:18

וינס‏H5127 ארם‏H758 מפני‏H6440 ישראל‏H3478 ויהרג‏H2026 דוד‏H1732
מארם‏H758 שבע‏H7651 מאות‏H3967 רכב‏H7393 וארבעים‏H705 אלף‏H505
פרשים‏H6571 ואת‏H853 שובך‏H7731 שר‏H8269 צבאו‏H6635 הכה‏H5221
וימת‏H4191 שם:‏H8033

- 1 Chronicles 19:18

מארם‏H758 דויד‏H1732 ויהרג‏H2026 ישראל‏H3478 מלפני‏H6440 ארם‏H758

איש‏H376 אלף‏H505 וארבעים‏H705 רכב‏H7393 אלפים‏H505 שבעת‏H7651

המית:‏H4191 הצבא‏H6635 שר‏H8269 שופך‏H7780 ואת‏H853 רגלי‏H7273

The Hebrew uses identical phrasing for both 2 Samuel 10:18 and 1 Chronicles 19:18, changing only the number in each (700 in the former and 7,000 in the latter). The phrase in question is as follows:

שבע מאות רכב וארבעים אלף

שבעת אלפים רכב וארבעים אלף

The term for "chariot" used in both verses is identical—H7393 (רֶכֶב / rekeb). It can mean "team, chariot, chariotry, mill-stone, riders." The fact that the same word was used in both instances likely indicates that the term had the same meaning in each, and the difference in the number was due to a scribal error.

(3) Response to the Problem of the Explanation

H7393 (רֶכֶב / rekeb) can mean both "chariot" and "riders" (charioteers). It is therefore possible that the author of 2 Samuel intended to write that 700 chariots were slain and the writer of 1 Chronicles meant to write that 7,000 charioteers were slain. While 10 riders in a chariot would be a high number, it is not unreasonable, since a squad typically consists of 8 or 9 soldiers. The translation of the KJV is thus not unreasonable.

4. Whether Jesus or Simon Carried Jesus's Cross

a) Overview

Dr. Philips writes that the "Gospel accounts vary regarding who carried the cross on which Jesus was supposed to have been crucified. In Matthew, Mark and Luke, it was Simon of Cyrene, and in John, it was Jesus" (p. 25).

It is true that in Matthew, Mark and Luke, Simon of Cyrene carried the cross:

> Mat 27:31 And when they had mocked Him, they took the robe off Him, put His own clothes on Him, and led Him away to be crucified. Mat 27:32 Now *as they came out*, they found a man of Cyrene, <u>Simon</u> by name. Him they <u>compelled to bear His cross</u>.

> Mark 15:20 And when they had mocked Him, they took the purple off Him, put His own clothes on Him, and led Him out to crucify

Him. Mark 15:21 Then they compelled a certain man, <u>Simon a Cyrenian</u>, the father of Alexander and Rufus, *as he was coming out of the country* and passing by, <u>to bear His cross</u>.

Luke 23:25 And he released to them the one they requested, who for rebellion and murder had been thrown into prison; but he delivered Jesus to their will. Luke 23:26 Now *as they led Him away*, they laid hold of a certain man, <u>Simon a Cyrenian</u>, who was coming from the country, and <u>on him they laid the cross</u> that he might bear it after Jesus.

However, in John, it was Jesus:

John 19:16 Then he delivered Him to them to be crucified. Then *they took Jesus and led Him away*. John 19:17 And <u>He, bearing His cross</u>, went out to a place called the Place of a Skull, which is called in Hebrew, Golgotha.

Matthew	Mark	Luke	John
Mat 27:31 And when they had mocked Him, they took the robe off Him, put His own clothes on Him,	Mark 15:20 And when they had mocked Him, they took the purple off Him, put His own clothes on Him,	Luke 23:25 And he released to them the one they requested, who for rebellion and murder had been thrown into prison; but he delivered Jesus to their will.	John 19:16 Then he delivered Him to them to be crucified.
and <u>led Him away</u> to be crucified.	and <u>led Him out</u> to crucify Him.	Luke 23:26 Now as they <u>led Him away</u>,	Then they took Jesus and <u>led Him away</u>.
Mat 27:32 Now as they came out, they found a man of Cyrene, Simon by name.	Mark 15:21 Then they compelled a certain man, Simon a Cyrenian, the	they laid hold of a certain man, Simon a Cyrenian,	John 19:17 And <u>He, bearing His cross</u>, went out to a place called the Place of a

	father of Alexander and Rufus,		Skull, which is called in Hebrew, Golgotha.
	as he was coming out of the country and passing by,	who was coming from the country,	
Him they compelled to bear His cross.	to bear His cross.	and on him they laid the cross that he might bear it <u>after</u> <u>Jesus</u>.	

b) Explanation

(1) Introduction

The traditional explanation is that both Jesus and Simon of Cyrene carried the cross. Matthew, Mark and Luke do not state that <u>only</u> Simon carried the cross; nor does John state that <u>only</u> Jesus carried the cross. John 19:17 simply states that Jesus bore his cross. Most likely, Jesus set off from the place of his conviction with the crossbeam on his shoulders. When he reached the city gates, he collapsed under the weight of the cross, following the physical trauma his body had experienced. At that point, the Roman soldiers ordered Simon to carry the cross beam.

(2) Attempted Harmonization

(a) Overview

In Matthew 27:31, we read that after the soldiers mocked Jesus and "took the robe off Him [and] put His own clothes on Him," they "led Him away to be crucified." Most likely, as they led him away to be crucified, they forced him to bear the crossbeam of his cross. Matthew 27:32 then states that "as they came out, they found a man of Cyrene, <u>Simon</u> by name." Matthew is likely referring to the soldier's exit from the city walls towards Golgatha. At that point, Matthew 27:32 states that the soldiers "compelled" Simon "to bear" Jesus's cross. Most likely, Jesus bore the cross from the place of his conviction to the city walls, at which point carrying the cross was shifted to Simon.

(b) Line-by-Line Account

(i) Mark

Matthew states:

> Mat 27:31 And when they had mocked Him, they took the robe off Him, put His own clothes on Him, and <u>led Him away to be crucified</u>.

These actions commenced in the city of Jerusalem, where Jesus was condemned.

> Mat 27:32 Now as they came out, they found a man of Cyrene, Simon by name. Him they compelled to bear His cross.

Then, as they "came out" of the city of Jerusalem, the soldiers compelled Simon of Cyrene to bear Jesus's cross, presumably because Jesus, in a weakened and traumatized physical state, was unable to bear the weight of the cross all the way to Golgotha.

(ii) Mark and Luke

Mark's and Luke's account agrees with Matthew's account, but they add one further detail: The soldiers ordered Simon to carry Jesus's cross as Simon was coming out of the country and passing by. Mark states "as he was coming out of the country and passing by" (Mark 15:21) and Luke states, "who was coming from the country" (Luke 23:26). This would be consistent with the view that Simon was compelled to bear Jesus's cross after Jesus reached Jerusalem's city walls and set out for Golgotha. After Jesus reached the city walls, he exited into the country towards Golgotha. It was at that time that the soldiers intercepted and recruited Simon, who was passing by in the country, to carry the cross.

(iii)John

John's account states:

> John 19:16 Then he delivered Him to them to be crucified. Then they took Jesus and <u>led Him away</u>.

> John 19:17 And He, <u>bearing His cross</u>, <u>went out to a place called the Place of a Skull</u>, which is called in Hebrew, Golgotha.

If the soldiers intercepted Simon in the country as he was passing by and had him bear the cross from the country (i.e., outside of the city gates) to Golgotha, then the account in John must be referring to Jesus's bearing the cross from the place of conviction in Jerusalem to the city walls.

(3) Jesus Did Not Bear the Cross to Golgotha Because of Physical Trauma

The physical trauma that Jesus underwent prior to being ordered to carry his cross in John 19:17 is recorded as follows:

- Luke 22:44 And being in agony, He prayed more earnestly. Then <u>His sweat became like great drops of blood</u> falling down to the ground.
- John 18:22 And when He had said these things, one of the officers who stood by struck Jesus with the palm of his hand, saying, "Do You answer the high priest like that?" John 18:23 Jesus answered him, "If I have spoken evil, bear witness of the evil; but if well, why do you strike Me?"
- Mark 14:65 Then some began to spit on Him, and to blindfold Him, and to beat Him, and to say to Him, "Prophesy!" And the officers struck Him with the palms of their hands.
- Mat 27:26 Then he released Barabbas to them; and when he had scourged Jesus, he delivered Him to be crucified.
- Mat 27:29 When they had twisted a crown of thorns, they put it on His head, and a reed in His right hand. And they bowed the knee before Him and mocked Him, saying, "Hail, King of the Jews!" Mat 27:30 Then they spat on Him, and took the reed and struck Him on the head. Mat 27:31 And when they had mocked Him, they took the robe off Him, put His own clothes on Him, and led Him away to be crucified.

Jesus started to carry the cross, but He simply could not bear it very far after all the physical trauma He bore. He collapsed. That is when the Romans drafted Simon of Cyrene to carry the cross the rest of the way.[5]

(4) Why Matthew, Mark and Luke, on the One Hand, and John, on the Other, Offer Discrepant Accounts of Who Bore the Cross

The population of Jerusalem during Passover would have swelled to a number higher than any normal week. Thus, it would have been virtually impossible for Matthew or John to follow Jesus every step of the way from conviction to crucifixion. Matthew recorded Roman

---

[5]   See   https://carm.org/bible-difficulties/matthew-mark/did-jesus-or-simon-cyrene-carry-cross.

officials ordering Simon the Cyrene to carry the crossbeam from outside the gates to Golgotha from his vantage point, whereas John recorded Jesus carrying the crossbeam through the city streets, from his own vantage point. It is possible that both Matthew and John were unable to follow Jesus the entire journey to Golgotha, and so each recorded only what he saw.[6]

This explanation would be consistent with the likelihood that John, one of the inner three of Jesus's apostles, would have been present at the time and place of Jesus's conviction.

(5) Bible Commentaries

(a) Albert Barnes' Notes on the Bible

Albert Barnes' Notes on the Bible makes this point. It states:

> John says that Jesus went forth "bearing his cross." Luke says Luk_23:26 that they laid the cross on Simon, that he might bear it after Jesus. There is no contradiction in these accounts. It was a part of the usual punishment of those who were crucified that they should bear their own cross to the place of execution. Accordingly, it was laid at first on Jesus, and he went forth, as John says, bearing it. Weak, however, and exhausted by suffering and watchfulness, he probably sunk under the heavy burden, and they laid hold of Simon that he might bear "one end" of the cross, as Luke says, "after Jesus." The cross was composed of two pieces of wood, one of which was placed upright in the earth, and the other crossed it after the form of the figure of a cross. The upright part was commonly so high that the feet of the person crucified were 2 or 3 feet from the ground.

(b) Adam Clarke's Commentary on the Bible

Adam Clarke's Commentary on the Bible states:

> In John, we are told Christ himself bore the cross, and this, it is likely, he did for a part of the way; but, being exhausted with the scourging and other cruel usage which he had received, he was found incapable of bearing it alone; therefore they obliged Simon, not, I think, to bear it entirely, but to assist Christ, by bearing a part of it. It was a constant practice among the Romans, to oblige

---

[6]   See   <https://answersingenesis.org/contradictions-in-the-bible/who-really-carried-the-cross-of-jesus/>.

criminal to bear their cross to the place of execution: insomuch that Plutarch makes use of it as an illustration of the misery of vice. "Every kind of wickedness produces its own particular torment, just as every malefactor, when he is brought forth to execution, carries his own cross." See Lardner's Credib. vol. i. p. 160.

(c) The NIV Study Bible

The NIV Study Bible note at Mark 15:21 states:

Men condemned to death were usually forced to carry a beam of the cross, often weighing 30 or 40 pounds, to the place of the crucifixion. Jesus started out by carrying his (see Jn 19:17), but he had been so weakened by flogging that Simon was pressed into service.

The NIV Study Bible note at John 19:17 further states:

Somewhere along the way Simon of Cyrene took Jesus's cross (Mk 15:21), probably because Jesus was weakened by the flogging.

5. Genealogy of Jesus Christ

a) Introduction

(1) Overview

Dr. Philips writes (p. 27-28):

When the genealogy of Jesus from David in Matthew 1:6-16 is compared to that of Luke 3:23-31, there are major discrepancies. Firstly, Jesus in Matthew has 26 parents between himself and David, but in Luke he has 41. Secondly, the names in both lists vary radically after David, and only two names are the same: Joseph, and Zorobabel. Both lists start off with Joseph, strangely enough, as the father of Jesus, but in Matthew, the author records Jesus' paternal grandfather as being Jacob, while in Luke he is Heli. If one were to accept the suggestion of some that one of the lists is actually the genealogy of Mary, it could not possibly account for any differences after their common ancestor David. Both lists meet again at Abraham and between David and Abraham most of the names are the same. However, in Matthew's list, Hezron's son's name is Ram, the father of Ammin' adab, while in Luke's list, Hezron's son's name is Ami whose son's name is Admin, the father of Ammin'adab.45

Consequently, between David and Abraham there are 12 forefathers in Matthew's list and 13 in Luke's list. T Visits to Jesus's Tomb Following the Crucifixion

(2) Matthew's Account

Matthew's account of the genealogy is as follows (Mat 1:2-16):

1. Mat 1:2 Abraham begot Isaac
2. Isaac begot Jacob
3. Jacob begot Judah and his brothers
4. Mat 1:3 Judah begot Perez and Zerah by Tamar
5. Perez begot Hezron
6. Hezron begot Ram
7. Mat 1:4 Ram begot Amminadab
8. Amminadab begot Nahshon
9. Nahshon begot Salmon
10. Mat 1:5 Salmon begot Boaz by Rahab
11. Boaz begot Obed by Ruth
12. Obed begot Jesse
13. Mat 1:6 and Jesse begot _David_ the king
14. _David_ the king begot Solomon by her who had been the wife of Uriah.
15. Mat 1:7 Solomon begot Rehoboam
16. Rehoboam begot Abijah
17. Abijah begot Asa
18. Mat 1:8 Asa begot Jehoshaphat
19. Jehoshaphat begot Joram
20. Joram begot Uzziah
21. Mat 1:9 Uzziah begot Jotham
22. Jotham begot Ahaz
23. Ahaz begot Hezekiah
24. Mat 1:10 Hezekiah begot Manasseh
25. Manasseh begot Amon
26. Amon begot Josiah
27. Mat 1:11 Josiah begot Jeconiah and his brothers about the time they were carried away to _Babylon_
28. Mat 1:12 And after they were brought to _Babylon_, Jeconiah begot Shealtiel
29. Shealtiel begot Zerubbabel
30. Mat 1:13 Zerubbabel begot Abiud

31. Abiud begot Eliakim
32. Eliakim begot Azor
33. Mat 1:14 Azor begot Zadok
34. Zadok begot Achim
35. Achim begot Eliud
36. Mat 1:15 Eliud begot Eleazar
37. Eleazar begot Matthan
38. Matthan begot Jacob
39. Mat 1:16 Jacob begot Joseph the husband of Mary
40. of whom was born Jesus who is called Christ.
-   Mat 1:17 So all the generations from Abraham to David are *fourteen generations*, from David until the captivity in Babylon are *fourteen generations*, and from the captivity in Babylon until the Christ are *fourteen generations*.

(3) Luke's Account (Luke 3:23-38)

Luke's account of the genealogy of Christ is as follows:

1. Luke 3:23 Now Jesus Himself began His ministry at about thirty years of age, being (as was supposed) the son of Joseph
2. *the son* of Heli,
3. Luke 3:24 the son of Matthat
4. the son of Levi
5. the son of Melchi
6. the son of Janna
7. the son of Joseph,
8. Luke 3:25 the son of Mattathiah
9. the son of Amos
10. the son of Nahum
11. the son of Esli
12. the son of Naggai
13. Luke 3:26 the son of Maath
14. the son of Mattathiah
15. the son of Semei
16. the son of Joseph
17. the son of Judah,
18. Luke 3:27 the son of Joannas
19. the son of Rhesa
20. the son of Zerubbabel
21. the son of Shealtiel

22. the son of Neri
23. Luke 3:28 the son of Melchi
24. the son of Addi
25. the son of Cosam
26. the son of Elmodam
27. the son of Er
28. Luke 3:29 the son of Jose
29. the son of Eliezer
30. the son of Jorim
31. the son of Matthat
32. the son of Levi
33. Luke 3:30 the son of Simeon
34. the son of Judah
35. the son of Joseph
36. the son of Jonan
37. the son of Eliakim
38. Luke 3:31 the son of Melea
39. the son of Menan
40. the son of Mattathah
41. the son of Nathan
42. the son of David
43. Luke 3:32 the son of Jesse
44. the son of Obed
45. the son of Boaz
46. the son of Salmon
47. the son of Nahshon
48. Luke 3:33 the son of Amminadab
49. the son of Ram
50. the son of Hezron
51. the son of Perez
52. the son of Judah
53. Luke 3:34 the son of Jacob
54. the son of Isaac
55. the son of Abraham
56. the son of Terah
57. the son of Nahor
58. Luke 3:35 the son of Serug
59. the son of Reu
60. the son of Peleg
61. the son of Eber

62. the son of Shelah
63. Luke 3:36 the son of Cainan
64. the son of Arphaxad
65. the son of Shem
66. the son of Noah
67. the son of Lamech
68. Luke 3:37 the son of Methuselah
69. the son of Enoch
70. the son of Jared
71. the son of Mahalalel
72. the son of Cainan
73. Luke 3:38 the son of Enosh
74. the son of Seth
75. the son of Adam
76. the son of God.

(4) Comparison

Matthew 1:2-16	*Luke (3:23-38)*
	God
	Adam
	Seth
	Enosh
	Cainan
	Mahalalel
	Jared
	Enoch
	Methuselah
	Lamech
	Noah
	Shem
	Arphaxad
	Cainan
	Shelah
	Eber

Matthew 1:2-16	Luke (3:23-38)
	Peleg
	Reu
	Luke 3:35 Serug
	Nahor
	Terah
Abraham	**Abraham**
Mat 1:2 Abraham begot Isaac	Isaac
Isaac begot Jacob	Luke 3:34 Jacob
Jacob begot Judah	Judah
Mat 1:3 Judah begot Perez	Perez
Perez begot Hezron	Hezron
Hezron begot Ram	Ram
Mat 1:4 Ram begot Amminadab	Luke 3:33 Amminadab
Amminadab begot Nahshon	Nahshon
Nahshon begot Salmon	Salmon
Mat 1:5 Salmon begot Boaz	Boaz
Boaz begot Obed	Obed
Obed begot Jesse	Luke 3:32 Jesse
Mat 1:6 Jesse begot **David**	**David**
David the king begot *Solomon* (of Bathsheba)	*Nathan* (of Bathsheba)
Mat 1:7 *Rehoboam*	*Mattathah*
Rehoboam begot Abijah	Menan
Asa	Melea
Mat 1:8 Jehoshaphat	Eliakim
Joram	Jonan
Uzziah	Joseph
Mat 1:9 Jotham	Judah
Ahaz	Simeon

Matthew 1:2-16	*Luke (3:23-38)*
Hezekiah	Luke 3:30 Levi
Mat 1:10 Manasseh	Matthat
Amon	Jorim
Josiah	Eliezer
Mat 1:11 Jeconiah about the time they were carried away to **Babylon**	Jose
Mat 1:12 And after they were brought to **Babylon**, Jeconiah begot Shealtiel	Luke 3:29 Er
Zerubbabel	Elmodan
Mat 1:13 *Abiud*	Cosam
Eliakim	Addi
Eliakim begot Azor	Melchi
Mat 1:14 Azor begot Zadok	Luke 3:28 Neri
Zadok begot Achim	Shealtiel
Achim begot Eliud	**Zerubbabel**
Mat 1:15 Eliud begot Eleazar	*Rhesa*
Eleazar begot Matthan	Joannas
Matthan begot Jacob	Luke 3:27 Judah
Mat 1:16 **Jacob** begot Joseph the husband of Mary	Joseph
of whom was born Jesus who is called Christ.	Semei
	Mattahiah
	Maath
	Luke 3:26 Naggai
	Esli
	Nahum
	Amos

Matthew 1:2-16	Luke (3:23-38)
	Mattathiah
	Luke 3:25 Joseph
	Janna
	Melchi
	Levi
	Matthat
	Luke 3:24 **Heli**
	Joseph
	Luke 3:23 Jesus [was supposed] the son of Joseph

b)   General Response

(1) Adam Clarke's *Commentary on the Bible*

Adam Clarke's *Commentary on the Bible* addresses this issue as follows:

> Matthew, in descending from Abraham to Joseph, the spouse of the blessed virgin, speaks of Sons properly such, by way of natural generation: Abraham begat Isaac, and Isaac begat Jacob, etc. But Luke, in ascending from the Savior of the world to God himself, speaks of sons either properly or improperly such: on this account he uses an indeterminate mode of expression, which may be applied to sons either *putatively* or *really* such. And Jesus himself began to be about thirty years of age, being, as was Supposed the son of Joseph - of Heli - of Matthat, etc. This receives considerable support from Raphelius's method of reading the original ων (ὡς ενομιζετο υἱος Ιωσηφ) του Ἡλι, being (when reputed the son of Joseph) the son of Heli, etc. That St. Luke does not always speak of sons properly such, is evident from the first and last person which he names: Jesus Christ was only the supposed son of Joseph, because Joseph was the husband of his mother Mary: and Adam, who is said to be the son of God, was such only by creation. After this observation it is next necessary to consider, that, in the genealogy described by St. Luke, there are two sons improperly such: i.e. two sons-in-law, instead of two sons. As the Hebrews never permitted

women to enter into their genealogical tables, whenever a family happened to end with a daughter, instead of naming her in the genealogy, they inserted her husband, as the son of him who was, in reality, but his father-in-law. This import, bishop Pearce has fully shown, νομιζεσθαι bears, in a variety of places - Jesus was considered according to law, or allowed custom, to be the son of Joseph, as he was of Heli. The two sons-in-law who are to be noticed in this genealogy are Joseph the son-in-law of Heli, whose own father was Jacob, Mat_1:16; and Salathiel, the son-in-law of Neri, whose own father was Jechonias: 1Ch_3:17, and Mat_1:12. This remark alone is sufficient to remove every difficulty. Thus it appears that Joseph, son of Jacob, according to St. Matthew, was son-in-law of Heli, according to St. Luke. And Salathiel, son of Jechonias, according to the former, was son-in-law of Neri, according to the latter. Mary therefore appears to have been the daughter of Heli; so called by abbreviation for Heliachim, which is the same in Hebrew with Joachim. Joseph, son of Jacob, and Mary; daughter of Heli, were of the same family: both came from Zerubbabel; Joseph from Abiud, his eldest son, Mat_1:13, and Mary by Rhesa, the youngest. See Luk_3:27. Salathiel and Zorobabel, from whom St. Matthew and St. Luke cause Christ to proceed, were themselves descended from Solomon in a direct line: and though St. Luke says that Salathiel was son of Neri, who was descended from Nathan, Solomon's eldest brother, 1Ch_3:5, this is only to be understood of his having espoused Nathan's daughter, and that Neri dying, probably, without male issues the two branches of the family of David, that of Nathan and that of Solomon, were both united in the person of Zerubbabel, by the marriage of Salathiel, chief of the regal family of Solomon, with the daughter of Neri, chief and heretrix of the family of Nathan. Thus it appears that Jesus, son of Mary, reunited in himself all the blood, privileges, and rights of the whole family of David; in consequence of which he is emphatically called, The son of David. It is worthy of being remarked that St. Matthew, who wrote principally for the Jews, extends his genealogy to Abraham through whom the promise of the Messiah was given to the Jews; but St. Luke, who wrote his history for the instruction of the Gentiles, extends his genealogy to Adam, to whom the promise of the Redeemer was given in behalf of himself and of all his posterity. See the notes on Mat 1:1, etc.

(2) Support for Clarke's Arguments: Luke Recounts the Names of the Putative Ascendants of Jesus; Matthew Recounts the Names of the Biological Descendants of Abraham

While Luke recounts the names of the putative ascendants of Jesus, Matthew recounts the names of the biological descendants of Abraham.

(a) Matthew Uses the Term "Begat" (γεννάω / gennáō)

This is made clear by the fact that Matthew uses the Greek "begat" (εγεννησεν/G1080) throughout the generational chain:

> 2 αβρααμG11 N-PRI εγεννησενG1080 V-AAI-3S τονG3588 T-ASM ισαακG2464 N-PRI ισαακG2464 N-PRI δεG1161 CONJ εγεννησενG1080 V-AAI-3S τονG3588 T-ASM ιακωβG2384 N-PRI ιακωβG2384 N-PRI δεG1161 CONJ εγεννησενG1080 V-AAI-3S τονG3588 T-ASM ιουδανG2455 N-ASM καιG2532 CONJ τουςG3588 T-APM αδελφουςG80 N-APM αυτουG846 P-GSM

Strong's Definitions defines the term γεννάω (gennáō) as "procreate (properly, of the father, but by extension of the mother); figuratively, to regenerate:—bear, beget, be born, bring forth, conceive, be delivered of, gender, make, spring."

(b) Luke Recounts the Putative and Actual Ascendants of Jesus, Often without Actually Stating the Word "Son"

Luke, on the other hand, does not use the term "begat." Rather, he references a chain of descendants by referring to "sons," but at times he omits the word "son" or references a "supposed" son, making it clear that his is not intended as a genealogical list. Rather, Luke recounts the names of both putative and actual ascendants of Jesus. The original manuscripts literally read as follows (Luke 3:23-24):

> Jesus "was supposed [*the*] son of Joseph, [*the son*] of Heli, the son of Matthat, [*the son*] of Levi, [*the son*] of Melchi

The items in brackets and italics are not found in the original text and were added by translators for the sake of clarity in the translation:

> AndG2532 JesusG2424 himselfG846 beganG756 to beG2258 aboutG5616 thirty years of age,G5144 G2094 beingG5607 (asG5613 was

supposed)G3543 theG3588 sonG5207 of Joseph,G2501 which was [*the son*] of Heli,G2242

καιG2532 CONJ αυτοςG846 P-NSM ηνG1510 V-IAI-3S οG3588 T-NSM ιησουςG2424 N-NSM ωσειG5616 ADV ετωνG2094 N-GPN τριακονταG5144 A-NUI αρχομενοςG756 V-PMP-NSM ωνG1510 V-PAP-NSM ωςG5613 ADV ενομιζετοG3543 V-IPI-3S υιοςG5207 N-NSM ιωσηφG2501 N-PRI τουG3588 T-GSM ηλιG2242 N-PRI

The original of Matthew 1:2-16, in contrast, quite literally lists generations. The English, "A begat B; and B begat C; and C begat D," etc., is present in the original Greek. For example:

Mat 1:2 AbrahamG11 begatG1080 Isaac;G2464 andG1161 IsaacG2464 begatG1080 Jacob;G2384 andG1161 JacobG2384 begatG1080 JudasG2455 andG2532 hisG846 brethren;G80

Mat 1:2 αβρααμG11 N-PRI εγεννησενG1080 V-AAI-3S τονG3588 T-ASM ισαακG2464 N-PRI ισαακG2464 N-PRI δεG1161 CONJ εγεννησενG1080 V-AAI-3S τονG3588 T-ASM ιακωβG2384 N-PRI ιακωβG2384 N-PRI δεG1161 CONJ εγεννησενG1080 V-AAI-3S τονG3588 T-ASM ιουδανG2455 N-ASM καιG2532 CONJ τουςG3588 T-APM αδελφουςG80 N-APM αυτουG846 P-GSM

(c) Luke's Account Includes Two Sons-In-Law

Clarke notes that "[a]s the Hebrews never permitted women to enter into their genealogical tables, whenever a family happened to end with a daughter, instead of naming her in the genealogy, they inserted her husband, as the son of him who was, in reality, but his father-in-law … The two sons-in-law who are to be noticed in this genealogy are *Joseph* the son-in-law of Heli, whose own father was Jacob, Mat 1:16; and *Salathiel* [Shealtiel], the son-in-law of Neri, whose own father was Jechonias [Jeconiah]: 1Ch 3:17, and Mat 1:12. Mary therefore appears to have been the daughter of Heli; so called by abbreviation for Heliachim, which is the same in Hebrew with Joachim."

Clarke continues: "Joseph, son of Jacob, and Mary, daughter of Heli, were of the same family: both came from Zerubbabel; Joseph from Abiud, [Zerubbabel's] eldest son, Mat 1:13, and Mary by Rhesa, the youngest [son of Zerubbabel]. See Luk 3:27."

c) Responses to Dr. Philip's Individual Claims

(1) Matthew States that Joseph's Father Was Jacob, but Luke States It Was Heli

Dr. Philips notes that "in Matthew, the author records Jesus' paternal grandfather as being Jacob, while in Luke he is Heli" (p. 27). Matthew states that Jacob begot Joseph (Mat 1:16), but Luke does not in fact state that Heli was Luke's father. Luke literally states that Jesus was "(as was supposed) the son of Joseph, of Heli" (Luke 3:23-24). The Greek does not include the words "son of" before Heli. The addition of the words was inserted by translators, since the literal Greek "of Heli" does not translate properly in English grammar. The Greek could have meant, and very likely did mean, that Joseph was the son-in-law of Heli, who was Mary's father Joachim, which is the same in Hebrew as Heliachim, which is abbreviated in Luke as "Heli." Therefore, there is no contradiction if reviewing the original Greek of Luke 3:23, which does not state that Joseph was the son of Heli.

(2) If Matthew Recounts Joseph's Genealogy and Luke Recounts Mary's, There Cannot Be Differences After David

Dr. Philip's writes that if "one were to accept the suggestion of some that one of the lists is actually the genealogy of Mary, it could not possibly account for any differences after their common ancestor David" (p. 27). If Dr. Philips means that the ascendants of David would need to be same in both Matthew and Luke, then there is no issue here, since Matthew and Luke both recount the ascendants of David as Jesse, son of Obed, son of Boaz, son of Salmon, son of Nahshon, son of Amminadab, son of Ram, son of Hezron, son of Perez, son of Judah, son of Jacob, son of Isaac, son of Abraham.

If, however, Dr. Philips means that the two lists would need to have the same descendants after David, this is not necessarily the case. Joseph could have very well been a descendent of David's son Solomon, while Mary was a descendent of David's son Nathan.

(3) Discrepancies Among the Descendants between Abraham and David

Dr. Philips writes that Matthew's and Luke's lists (p. 27-28):

> meet again at Abraham and between David and Abraham most of the names are the same. However, in Matthew's list, Hezron's son's name is Ram, the father of Ammin'adab, while in Luke's list, Hezron's son's name is Arni whose son's name is Admin, the father of Ammin'adab. Consequently, between David and Abraham there are 12 forefathers in Matthew's list and 13 in Luke's list.

Because there is some truth to this claim based on which translations of Luke are used, we examine Dr. Philips' claim under "Discrepancies in Manuscripts Recounting Jesus's Genealogy in Luke 3:33," under "Points that are True, but Insignificant," below.

6. Contradictions in the Visit to Jesus's Tomb

a) Overview

Dr. Philips writes (p. 26):

> After Jesus' 'crucifixion', the Gospel accounts differ as to who visited his tomb, when the visit took place, as well as the state of the tomb when it was visited. The Gospels of Matthew, Luke and John state that the visit took place before sunrise, while the Gospel of Mark states that it was after sunrise. In another three Gospels (Mark, Luke and John) the women found the stone door of the tomb rolled away, but in one (Matthew) the tomb was closed until an angel descended before them and rolled it away.

b) When the Visit Took Place

Dr. Philips writes that "[t]he Gospels of Matthew, Luke and John state that the visit took place before sunrise, while the Gospel of Mark states that it was after sunrise" (p. 26).

Dr. Philips is mistaken with respect to the account of Matthew and Luke. They do not state that the visit took place before sunrise. Rather, they state that Mary Magdalene arrived to the tomb when the first day started to dawn / very early in the morning:

> Mat 28:1 Now after the Sabbath, <u>as the first day of the week began to dawn</u>, Mary Magdalene and the other Mary came to see the tomb.

Luke 24:1 Now on the first day of the week, <u>very early in the morning</u>, they, and certain other women with them, came to the tomb bringing the spices which they had prepared.

In this respect, Matthew and Luke are consistent with Mark, which states that the women came to the tomb when the sun had risen.

Mark 16:1 Now when the Sabbath was past, Mary Magdalene, Mary the mother of James, and Salome bought spices, that they might come and anoint Him. Mark 16:2 Very early in the morning, on the first day of the week, <u>they came to the tomb when the sun had risen</u>.

This is consistent with Matthew and Luke, since the time that the sun had risen is the time that the day begins to dawn (Mat 28:1), which is very early in the morning (Luke 24:1).

There is, however, a difference in the account in John, which states that Mary Magdalene went to the tomb when it was still dark:

John 20:1 Now the first day of the week Mary Magdalene <u>went</u> to the tomb early, <u>while it was still dark</u>, and saw that the stone had been taken away from the tomb.

However, there is not necessarily a contradiction. John was likely referring to when Mary *went* to the tomb, whereas Matthew, Mark, and Luke were referring to when Mary arrived (*i.e.*, "came") to the tomb. It is entirely conceivable that Mary set off to the tomb while it was still dark, as John conveys, and that she arrived at dawn, just as the sun had risen, as Matthew, Mark, and Luke convey.

c) State of the Tomb When It Was Visited

Dr. Philips writes that in "three Gospels (Mark, Luke and John) the women found the stone door of the tomb rolled away, but in one (Matthew) the tomb was closed until an angel descended before them and rolled it away" (p. 26).

Dr. Philips is again mistaken in his account of the state of the tomb in Mark, Luke, and John versus that in Matthew. Matthew does not explicitly state that the women found the tomb closed until an angel descended and rolled it away; nor do Mark, Luke, and John state that the women found the stone rolled away when they arrived. Matthew simply states that an angel rolled away the stone, without making any reference as to whether this occurred before or after the women arrived. It is entirely conceivable that the stone had been rolled away by the time Mary arrived. The text states only as follows:

> Mat 28:1 Now after the Sabbath, as the first day of the week began to dawn, Mary Magdalene and the other Mary came to see the tomb.

> Mat 28:2 And behold, there was a great earthquake; for an angel of the Lord descended from heaven, and came and rolled back the stone from the door, and sat on it.

> Mat 28:3 His countenance was like lightning, and his clothing as white as snow.

> Mat 28:4 And the guards shook for fear of him, and became like dead men.

> Mat 28:5 But the angel answered and said to the women, "Do not be afraid, for I know that you seek Jesus who was crucified.

It is entirely within the realm of the possible that as the women set out to see the tomb, an angel descended from heaven and rolled back the stone, causing fear to overcome the guards. Then, when the women arrived, the angel said to them to not be afraid, after the stone had already been rolled away. There would thus be no contradiction.

7. Fate of Judas Iscariot

a) Overview

Dr. Philips writes that the "New Testament accounts vary regarding the fate of Judas Iscariot and the money he received for betraying Jesus. In Matthew, he hung himself, while in Acts, he fell in a field and died there" (p. 27).

Matthew 27:5 states that Judas Iscariot died by hanging, but Acts 1:18 states he died by falling and bursting open:

-   Mat 27:5 Then he threw down the pieces of silver in the temple and departed, and went and hanged himself.
-   Acts 1:18 Now this man purchased a field with the wages of iniquity; and falling headlong, he burst open in the middle and all his entrails gushed out.

b) Proposed Explanation

Matthew's Gospel account and Luke's account in Acts are two different viewpoints of the same event:
- Matthew tells us that Judas died by hanging.
- Luke, being a doctor, gives us a graphic description of what occurred following the hanging (*i.e.*, Judas fell, burst open and his organs spilled.

It is possible that Judas hanged himself and he fell down, with his entrails spilling out. Most likely, if a person falls and his entrails spill out, he will probably not survive the event. However, if a person hangs himself, he might survive the event (e.g., in the event he rescues himself by climbing up the robe or untying it, or in the event the rope or branch on which he is hung snaps before the person dies). Therefore, Judas likely hanged himself before he fell and had his entrails spill. While it is possible that Judas could have survived the hanging and then fell, what is more likely is that while he was hanging, he fell following a break in the rope or the branch from which he hung breaking). The fact that he could have hanged himself before falling from the rope indicates that the apparent discrepancies between the accounts in Matthew and Luke are not necessarily contradictions.

8. Jesus is Crucified on 15 Nisan in the Synoptic Gospels and on 14 Nisan in the Gospel of John

a) Overview

Dr. Philips writes that in the Synoptic Gospels, "Jesus is crucified on 15 Nisan," but in the Gospel of John, "Jesus is crucified on 14 Nisan, the day of the Jewish Passover sacrifice" (p. 53).

It appears that:
- in the Synoptic Gospels, the Last Supper is held on Passover, just after sunset on 14 Nisan and into the evening of 15 Nisan. He is then crucified the next day, 15 Nisan, which is the first day of the Feast of Unleavened Bread.
- in John, Jesus is crucified on the Preparation day of Passover, which would have been held on Saturday. Therefore, the Friday of Jesus's crucifixion would have been 14 Nisan, with Passover falling the next day (Saturday).

b) Introduction to Passover and the Feast of Unleavened Bread

Passover is on 14 Nisan. It is celebrated with a Passover seder beginning on the evening after 14 Nisan, which is the evening of 15 Nisan just after sunset on 14 Nisan. The Passover seder is a Jewish ritual feast that marks the beginning of Passover.

The Feast of Unleavened Bread extends over seven days. The first and last days are high Sabbaths in which no work is undertaken. The instruction to observe the Feast of Unleavened Bread was given in relation to Passover, which the Feast is a continuation of (Lev 23:4-8):

> Lev 23:4 These are the feasts of the Lord, holy convocations which you shall proclaim at their appointed times.
>
> Lev 23:5 *On the fourteenth day of the first month at twilight is the Lord's Passover*.
>
> Lev 23:6 *And on the fifteenth day of the same month is the Feast of Unleavened Bread to the Lord; seven days you must eat unleavened bread*.
>
> Lev 23:7 On the first day you shall have a holy convocation; you shall do no customary work on it.
>
> Lev 23:8 But you shall offer an offering made by fire to the Lord for seven days. The seventh day shall be a holy convocation; you shall do no customary work on it.

According to Chabad.org, following twilight on 14 Nisan, when the Passover was eaten, was technically the beginning of a new day, which was 15 Nisan. However, in the Jewish calendar, that evening of 15 Nisan was considered to be an *extension* of 14 Nisan[7]:

> Also note that, in a certain sense, the celebration of the 15th is considered to be an extension of the 14th. How so? With regard to sacrifices, the verse states, "And the flesh of his thanksgiving peace offering shall be eaten on the day it is offered up; he shall not leave any of it over until morning." In other words, if you were given one day to eat an offering, the day consisted of the daytime followed by its night (unlike all other purposes, for which Jewish calendar days consist of the night followed by the day). Thus, as far as sacrifices

---

[7] "Why Is Passover on Nissan 15, Not Nissan 14?" available at <https://www.chabad.org/holidays/passover/pesach_cdo/aid/3283921/jewish/Why-Is-Passover-on-Nissan-15-Not-Nissan-14.htm>.

are concerned, the night after a sacrifice is brought is an extension of the day it is brought.

Therefore, when it comes to the celebration of the Passover sacrifice, while it was eaten on the 15th, it was considered to be the same day as the 14th.

We can thus conclude that Passover was eaten following twilight on 14 Nisan and at the beginning of 15 Nisan, with the Feast of Unleavened Bread then following for 7 days.

c) *Scriptural Overview*

(1) Chronological Overview of the Gospel Accounts
- The Last Supper (Thursday)
  o Matthew 26:17-29
  o Mark 14:12-25
  o Luke 22:7-20
  o John 13:1-38

- Gethsemane (Thursday)
  o Matthew 26:36-46
  o Mark 14:32-42
  o Luke 22:40-46

- Jesus' Arrest and Trial (Thursday night and Friday)
  o Matthew 26:47-27:26
  o Mark 14:43-15:15
  o Luke 22:47-23:25
  o John 18:2-19:16

- Jesus' Crucifixion and Death (Friday)
  o Matthew 27:27-26
  o Mark 15:16-41
  o Luke 23:26-49
  o John 19:17-30

(2) Matthew's Account

(a) Verses that State that Jesus Was Crucified on the First Day of the Feast of Unleavened Bread

The following verses suggest that Jesus was crucified on 15 Nisan, the first day of the Feast of Unleavened Bread:

> Jesus said to His disciples that <u>the Passover was after two days</u> and He would be crucified (Mat 26:1-2).

> On the <u>first day of the Feast of Unleavened Bread,</u>[8] <u>the disciples came to Jesus, asking where He wanted them to prepare to eat the Passover</u> (Mat 26:17). He said to go into the city to a certain man and say to him that Jesus would keep the <u>Passover</u> at his house with his disciples (Mat 26:18). The disciples did as Jesus had directed and they prepared the <u>Passover</u> (Mat 26:19).

> <u>When it was evening</u>, He sat down with the twelve disciples (Mat 26:20). He said that the disciple who dipped his hand with Him in the dish would betray Him (Mat 26:21-3). Judas asked, Is it I? Jesus replied that it was (Mat 26:25). Jesus broke bread and gave it and the cup to the disciples (Mat 26:26-29).

> They then went out to the Mount of Olives (Mat 26:30) and Jesus came with them to Gethsemane and said to the disciples to sit while He goes and prays (Mat 26:36). Then Judas appeared with a great multitude with swords and clubs (Mat 26:47). Then they took Jesus (Mat 26:50) away to Caiaphas, the high priest (Mat 26:57), where he was charged.

Jesus is arrested and then crucified the following day, which was a continuation of 15 Nisan in the Jewish calendar.

(b) Verses that State that Jesus was Crucified on the Day of Preparation

Matthew states that the day of the crucifixion was the Preparation Day and that the day after the Preparation Day the chief priests and Pharisees asked Pilate to secure the tomb:

> On the next day, <u>which followed the Day of Preparation</u>, the chief priests and Pharisees gathered together and said to Pilate, We remember, while Jesus was alive, He said He will rise after three days; therefore, command that the tomb be secured until the third day, lest His disciples steal His body (Mat 27:62-64).

---

[8] Matthew seems to be speaking of Passover, but he refers to it as the "Feast of Unleavened Bread."

This implies that Jesus was crucified on the Preparation Day.

(3) Mark's Account

(a) Verses that State that Jesus Was Crucified on the First Day of the Feast of Unleavened Bread

The following verses indicate that Jesus was crucified on the first day of the Feast of Unleavened Bread:

> On the first day of Unleavened Bread [Passover], when they killed the Passover lamb, Jesus' disciples asked Him where He wanted them to go and prepare to eat the Passover (Mark 14:12). Jesus sent two of His disciples into the city (Mark 14:13) and to request from the owner of a house the guest room for Jesus to eat the Passover with His disciples (Mark 14:14). He would show them a large upper room to make ready for them (Mark 14:15). The disciples went to the city and prepared the Passover (Mark 14:16).

> They sung a hymn and went to the Mount of Olives (Mark 14:26), where Jesus predicted that before the rooster crows twice, Peter would deny Him three times (Mark 14:30). Then they came to Gethsemane, where Jesus told His disciples to sit while he prays (Mark 14:32).

> While Jesus was speaking, Judas and the chief priests, scribes and elders came with a great multitude with swords and clubs and arrested Jesus (Mark 14:43-51). He was brought before the Sanhedrin, where He admitted to being the Son of God (Mark 14:53-64).

Jesus is then crucified the following day, which was a continuation of 15 Nisan on the Jewish calendar.

(b) Verses that State that Jesus was Crucified on the Day of Preparation

Mark states that the evening of the crucifixion was the Preparation Day before the Sabbath (Mark 15:42):

> When evening had come, because it was the Preparation Day, that is, the day before the Sabbath (Mark 15:42), Joseph of Arimathea, a prominent council member, who was waiting for the kingdom of God, went in to Pilate and asked for the body of Jesus (Mark 15:43). Pilate granted the body to Joseph (Mark 15:45). Joseph bought fine linen, took Him down, wrapped Him in the linen, laid Him in a

tomb and rolled a stone against the door of the tomb (Mark 15:46). Mary Magdalene and Mary the mother of Joses observed where He was laid (Mark 15:47).

This implies that Jesus was crucified on either the Preparation Day (Friday) or the Preparation Day to Passover. However, the Bible does not make a reference to a "Preparation Day" for Passover, and so this latter option is unlikely.

(4) Luke's Account

(a) Verses that State that Jesus was Crucified on the First Day of the Feast of Unleavened Bread

The following verses indicate that the Last Supper was the Passover seder and Jesus was crucified on the first day of the Feast of Unleavened Bread:

> As the Feast of Unleavened Bread, which is called Passover, drew near (Luke 22:1), the chief priests and scribes sought to kill Jesus (Luke 22:2). Satan entered Judas Iscariot (Luke 22:3), who went to the chief priests and officers of the temple guard to betray Jesus in the absence of the crowds (Luke 22:4-6).

> The Day of Unleavened Bread [Passover], when the Passover lamb had to be sacrificed, then came (Luke 22:7). He sent Peter and John to go and prepare the Passover so that they may eat (Luke 22:8). He told them that when they entered the city, they would meet a man carrying a pitcher of water and to follow him into the house that he enters (Luke 22:10) and to prepare the Passover in the guest room (Luke 22:11-13).

> Jesus sat down with the twelve Apostles (Luke 22:14) and said that He fervently desired to eat the Passover with them before He suffered (Luke 22:15) and that He will no longer eat of it until it is fulfilled in the kingdom of God (Luke 22:16). He gave them the cup (Luke 22:17) and said He would not drink of the fruit of the vine again until the kingdom of God comes (Luke 22:18). He broke the bread and gave it to them, saying, This is My body given for you; do this in remembrance of Me (Luke 22:19). He also took the cup and said, This is the new covenant in My blood, which is poured out for you (Luke 22:20).

Jesus and His disciples went to the Mount of Olives (Luke 22:39). Then Judas appeared with a multitude and had Jesus arrested (Luke 22:47-53). They took Jesus to the home of the high priest.

According to Luke, the last supper was the Passover Seder, and Jesus represented the Passover sacrificial lamb, whose body and blood was given for His followers. Jesus, following His arrest, was crucified the following day, which was a continuation of 15 Nisan in the Jewish calendar.

(b) Verses that State that Jesus was Crucified on the Day of Preparation

According to Luke, Joseph took Jesus's body down and buried it on the Preparation Day of the Sabbath:

> Jesus was crucified (Luke 23:26) and died on the cross (Luke 24:44-49). A man named Joseph asked for Jesus' body (Luke 23:50-52). He took the body down, wrapped it in linen and laid it in a tomb (Luke 23:53). That day was the Preparation and the Sabbath drew near (Luke 23:54).

This implies that Jesus was crucified on the Preparation Day, which would have been a Friday.

(5) John's Account

According to John, Jesus was crucified on the Preparation Day:

- John states, "Now before the Feast of the Passover, when Jesus knew that His hour had come that He should depart from this world to the Father, having loved His own who were in the world, He loved them to the end. And supper being ended, the devil having already put it into the heart of Judas Iscariot, Simon's son, to betray Him" (John 13:1-2). It is unclear whether this meal was the Passover meal or a meal "before the Feast of the Passover" (John 13:1).
- Jesus was arrested on Thursday evening and the Jews led Jesus from Caiaphas to the palace of the Roman governor in the early morning [on Friday], but the Jews did not enter the palace to avoid ceremonial uncleanliness and to be able to eat the Passover (John 18:28), which would have presumably been on Saturday, with the Passover seder eaten on Friday evening.
- Pilate came out to the Jews and questioned them and then questioned Jesus, ultimately concluding that he found no fault with Jesus (John 18:29-38), yet the Jews cried out against Jesus

(John 19:12). Pilate brought Jesus out and sat down in the judgment seat (John 19:13). "[I]t was the <u>Preparation Day of the Passover</u>, and about the sixth hour" (John 19:14).[9]

- Pilate delivered Jesus to be crucified and the soldiers took hold of Him (John 19:16). The soldiers crucified Jesus (John 19:23) on <u>Friday, the Preparation Day</u>.

- "[B]ecause it was the <u>Preparation Day</u>, that the bodies should not remain on the cross on the Sabbath (for that Sabbath was a high day), the Jews asked Pilate that their legs might be broken, and that they might be taken away" (John 19:31).

John states the following:

> It was just before the <u>Passover</u> feast (John 13:1). The evening meal was being served (John 13:2) and Jesus washed the feet of His Apostles (John 13:4-11).

> Jesus went out with His disciples over the Brook Kidron, where there was a garden (John 18:1). Judas, having received a detachment of troops and officers from the chief priests and Pharisees, came there with torches and weapons (John 18:3). Jesus was arrested (John 18:12). They led Him away to Annas, the father-in-law of Caiaphas, the high priest that year (John 18:13).

> Then the Jews led Jesus from Caiaphas to the palace of the Roman governor and it was early morning [Friday], but the Jews did not enter the palace to avoid ceremonial uncleanliness and to be able to eat the Passover (John 18:28). Pilate came out to the Jews and questioned them and then questioned Jesus, ultimately concluding that he found no fault with Jesus (John 18:29-38). He offered to release Jesus or Barabbas, but they chose for Barabbas to be released (John 18:39-40).

> The Jews cried out, saying that if Pilate released Jesus, he was against Caesar, for Jesus made Himself a King (John 19:12). When Pilate heard this, he brought Jesus out and sat down in the judgment seat (John 19:13). It was the Preparation Day of the Passover at about the sixth hour (John 19:14).

---

[9] The sixth hour could mean noon or midnight, but if John used the supposed Roman time, it would mean 6:00 am or 6:00 pm.

Pilate delivered Jesus to be crucified and the soldiers took hold of Him (John 19:16). The soldiers crucified Jesus (John 19:23). Jesus declared, It is finished, and gave up His spirit (John 19:30).

Because it was the Preparation Day, so that the bodies not remain on the cross on the Sabbath (for that Sabbath was a high day), the Jews asked Pilate to have the legs broken and the bodies taken down (John 19:31).

d) Explanation: "Passover" Is Used Interchangeably with "Feast of Unleavened Bread"

(1) GotQuestions.org Explanation

According to GotQuestions.org,[10]

> One objection to the above chronology is based on John 18:28, which says, "The Jewish leaders took Jesus from Caiaphas to the palace of the Roman governor. By now it was early morning, and to avoid ceremonial uncleanness they did not enter the palace, because they wanted to be able to eat the Passover." At first glance, it seems that, whereas Jesus had eaten the Passover the night before, the Jewish leaders had not yet eaten the Passover—they still "wanted to be able to eat" it after Jesus was arrested. To reconcile this verse with the Synoptic narratives, we must remember this: Passover was the first day of the week-long Feast of Unleavened Bread.

> The Feast (or Festival) of Unleavened Bread (Chag HaMatzot) lasted for a full week, from Nissan 15 to Nissan 22. The first day of Unleavened Bread coincided with the day of Passover. Because of the close relation between Passover and the Feast of Unleavened Bread, the whole week was sometimes referred to as "Passover." The two holidays were (and still are) considered a single celebration. This explains John 18:28. *The Jewish leaders had already eaten the Passover proper, but there still remained other sacrifices to be made and meals to be eaten.* They were unwilling to defile themselves (Pilate's palace contained leaven) because it would disqualify them from participating in the remainder of the week's ceremonies (see Leviticus 23:8).

---

[10] "If Jesus was crucified on the Day of Preparation, why had He already eaten the Passover meal?" available at <https://www.gotquestions.org/Day-of-Preparation.html>.

The book of Chronicles confirms that there were other meals eaten throughout the week of the Feast of Unleavened Bread:

> 2Ch 30:13 Now many people, a very great assembly, gathered at Jerusalem to keep the Feast of Unleavened Bread in the second month.
>
> 2Ch 30:14 They arose and took away the altars that were in Jerusalem, and they took away all the incense altars and cast them into the Brook Kidron.
>
> 2Ch 30:15 Then they slaughtered the Passover lambs on the fourteenth day of the second month. The priests and the Levites were ashamed, and sanctified themselves, and brought the burnt offerings to the house of the Lord.
>
> 2Ch 30:16 They stood in their place according to their custom, according to the Law of Moses the man of God; the priests sprinkled the blood received from the hand of the Levites.
>
> 2Ch 30:17 For there were many in the assembly who had not sanctified themselves; therefore the Levites had charge of the slaughter of the Passover lambs for everyone who was not clean, to sanctify them to the Lord.
>
> 2Ch 30:18 For a multitude of the people, many from Ephraim, Manasseh, Issachar, and Zebulun, had not cleansed themselves, yet they ate the Passover contrary to what was written. But Hezekiah prayed for them, saying, "May the good Lord provide atonement for everyone
>
> 2Ch 30:19 who prepares his heart to seek God, the Lord God of his fathers, though he is not cleansed according to the purification of the sanctuary."
>
> 2Ch 30:20 And the Lord listened to Hezekiah and healed the people.
>
> 2Ch 30:21 So the children of Israel who were present at Jerusalem kept the Feast of Unleavened Bread seven days with great gladness; and the Levites and the priests praised the Lord day by day, singing to the Lord, accompanied by loud instruments.
>
> 2Ch 30:22 And Hezekiah gave encouragement to all the Levites who taught the good knowledge of the Lord; and they ate

throughout the feast seven days, offering peace offerings and making confession to the Lord God of their fathers.

(2) Brant Pitre's Explanation

Moreover, Footnote 68 on page 214 of Brant Pitre's *Jesus and the Jewish Roots of the Eucharist* states:

> I should note here that many modern scholars doubt that the Last Supper was in fact a Jewish Passover meal, despite the explicit testimony of Matthew, Mark, and Luke. This doubt is primarily rooted in an apparent chronological contradiction between John's Gospel and the Synoptics. For an overview of the problem, see Jeremias, *The Eucharistic Words of Jews*, 15- 88. In a longer study on Jesus and the Last Supper still in preparation (Grand Rapids: Eerdmans, forthcoming), I will argue that the apparent contradiction is based on a misinterpretation of the word Passover in John's Gospel, and that all four Gospels do in fact identify the Last Supper as a Passover meal. For this solution, see e.g., Craig L. Blomberg, The Historical Reliability of John's Gospel: Issues & Commentary) (Downers Grove, Ill.: InterVarsity, 2001), 193-94, 238-39, 246-47; Barry D. Smith, "The Chronology of the Last Supper," Westminster Theological Journal 53 (1991): 29-45; C. C. Torrey, "The Date of the Crucifixion According to the Fourth Gospel," Journal of Biblical Literature 50 (1931): 227-41; idem, "In the Fourth Gospel the Last Supper Was a Passover Meal," Jewish Quarterly Review 42 (1951-52): 237-50; Cornelius a Lapide, SJ., Commentary on the Four Gospels, 4 volumes (Fitzwilliam, N.H.: Loreto, 2008 [orig. ca. 1637]), 2:522-26; 4:512- 513; Thomas Aquinas, Summa Theologica, Part III, Q. 46, An. 9.

Brant Pitre's footnote focuses on the fact that John did not mean to circumscribe his use of the term "Passover" in his Gospel to the Thursday of 14 Nisan. Rather, he uses it more broadly:

- John states that the Jews did not enter the palace to avoid ceremonial uncleanliness and to be able to eat the <u>Passover</u> (John 18:28). Here, John is conflating Passover with the Feast of Unleavened Bread. On the evening of 15 Nisan, the Friday after Passover, the Jews would have had another meal, and it was this meal to which John was referring, though that day was not technically Passover as narrowly defined in Leviticus 23:5.

- John states that it was the <u>Preparation Day of the Passover</u> at about the sixth hour (John 19:14). Again, John is not referring to 14 Nisan, but rather, to the preparation day of the week of Passover, which would have bene the preparation day of the weekly Sabbath. This is because by the time of Jesus' coming, Passover and the Feast of Unleavened Bread were conflated, and referring to one referring to another. John could have just has easily written, "It was the Preparation Day of the Sabbath of the Feast of Unleavened Bread."
- John states that because it was the <u>Preparation Day</u>, so that the bodies not remain on the cross on the Sabbath (for that Sabbath was a high day), the Jews asked Pilate to have the legs broken and the bodies taken down (John 19:31). However, John does not specify that it was the Preparation Day of Passover. Here, Preparation Day would have been referring to the preparation day of the weekly Sabbath (*i.e.*, the Friday before the Sabbath).

(3) The Conflation of Passover and the Feast of Unleavened Bread as per Melanie J. Wright

In *Studying Judaism: The Critical Issues*, Melanie J. Wright writes:

> At the same time, since the destruction of the Jerusalem temple meant that sacrifices were no longer possible, they shifted emphasis from the lamp to the unleavened bread (matzah) as the primary symbol of the holiday.

This implies that the shift would have occurred after the destruction of the first Jewish template (Solomon's temple) in 586 BC, or possibly following the disrepair of the second temple (Zerubbabel's temple) in 20 BC or the destruction of the third temple (Herod's temple) in 70 AD, which was destroyed in 586 BC by the Babylonians under Nebuchadnezzar, when they burned Jerusalem.

(4) Current Usage

One Chabad[11] Jew that this author consulted confirmed that when modern Jews in America refer to Passover, they are not referring to 14 Nisan only. Rather, they are referring to the entire 8-week holiday consisting of both Passover and the Feast of Unleavened Bread. He wrote, "Passover refers to all 8 days." He further stated that modern Jews no longer use the term "Feast of Unleavened Bread." Professor Michael

---

[11] Chabad is an Orthodox Jewish Hasidic movement.

Satlow reiterates this idea in his post, "Passover and the Festival of Matzot: Synthesizing Two Holidays."[12] He writes:

> The holiday that today we call Passover had its origins as two separate holidays, Passover proper and the Festival of Unleavened Bread, chag ha-matzot.

Professor Satlow therefore confirms that today, what is called Passover actually combined both Passover and the Feast of Unleavened Bread. As discussed below, it appears that this was the case as early as the days of Jesus, if not earlier.

(5) Further Scriptural Support

So far, we have attempted to explain the apparent contradiction by arguing that the reference to the Jews' eating the Passover in John 18:28 should not be read narrowly as referring to the Passover meal following sunset on 14 Nisan, but rather, to both Passover and the Feast of Unleavened Bread more broadly. The Synoptic Evangelists used the term "Passover" to refer to both Passover and the Feast of Unleavened Bread, which, by the time of Jesus, had become interchangeable terms. The Evangelists used the terms "Passover" and "Feast of Unleavened Bread" interchangeably:

- Matthew states that on the first day of the "Feast of Unleavened Bread," the disciples came to Jesus, asking where He wanted them to prepare to eat the Passover (Mat 26:17). However, it could not have been the first day of the Feast of Unleavened Bread when the disciples came to Jesus because the Jews prepare the Passover on Passover, which is 14 Nisan, not on the Feast of Unleavened Bread, which is 15 Nisan. Therefore, by "Feast of Unleavened Bread," John must have been referring to Passover.

- Mark states that on the first day of "Unleavened Bread," when they killed the Passover lamb, Jesus' disciples asked Him where He wanted them to go and prepare to eat the Passover (Mark 14:12). Again, it could not have been the first Day of the Feast of Unleavened Bread (15 Nisan) when the Passover was prepared; the Passover is prepared on Passover (14 Nisan) to be eaten after

---

[12] "Passover and the Festival of Matzot: Synthesizing Two Holidays," TheTorah.com, available at <https://www.thetorah.com/article/passover-and-the-festival-of-matzot-synthesizing-two-holidays>.

twilight on 14 Nisan. Mark is therefore conflating Passover with the Feast of Unleavened Bread.

- Luke states that "the Feast of Unleavened Bread drew near, which is called Passover" (Luke 22:1). He further states "then came the Day of Unleavened Bread, when the Passover must be killed" (Luke 22:7). Again, the Passover lamb is killed on Passover, not on the Feast of Unleavened Bread, which follows Passover. Luke is conflating the two holidays.

Moreover, other books throughout the Old and New Testaments refer to Passover and the Feast of Unleavened Bread interchangeably:

- Ezekiel states, "In the first month, on the fourteenth day of the month, you shall observe the *Passover*, a feast of *seven days; unleavened bread shall be eaten*" (Eze 45:21).
- Acts 12:3-4 states, "And because he saw that it pleased the Jews, he proceeded further to seize Peter also. Now it was during the *Days of Unleavened Bread*. So when he had arrested him, he put him in prison, and delivered him to four squads of soldiers to keep him, intending to bring him before the people after *Passover*."

(6) How to Properly Read References to "Passover" in John

On the basis of the foregoing, we should not read the references to "Passover" in John as strictly referring to Passover proper; rather, we should read these as references to Passover and the Feast of Unleavened Bread as a continuous, eight-day holiday that began on 14 Nisan and concluded on 21 Nisan. In this light, we can read the following verses from John in the following ways:

(a) The Jews Eating the Passover

Jesus was arrested on Thursday evening and the Jews led Jesus from Caiaphas to the palace of the Roman governor in the early morning [on Friday], but the Jews did not enter the palace to avoid ceremonial uncleanliness and to be able to eat the Passover (John 18:28).

Here, John is not referring to the Passover meal that would have been eaten after twilight on 14 Nisan (Thursday evening), but rather, to one of the meals of the Feast of Unleavened Bread, which would have been celebrated throughout the week of 15-21 Nisan. Leviticus states that for seven days during the Feast of Unleavened Bread, unleavened bread must be eaten (Lev 23:6). Numbers states that during the Feast of Unleavened Bread, unleavened bread shall be eaten for seven days (Num

28:17). Both books refer to the Jews eating unleavened bread throughout the week, so there were meals that would have been eaten during the week in accordance with the scriptural mandate to eat unleavened bread.

Numbers 28:16-25 describes the sacrifices to be offered on each day of the Feast of Unleavened Bread as follows:

- On the first day you shall present an offering made by fire as a burnt offering to the Lord: two young bulls, one ram, and seven lambs in their first year and without blemish (Num 28:19).
- With each bull offer a grain offering of three-tenths of an ephah of flour mixed with oil; with the ram, two-tenths (Num 28:20) and with each of the seven lambs, one-tenth (Num 28:21)
- One goat as a sin offering (Num 28:22).
- You shall offer the food of the offering made by fire daily for seven days, as a sweet aroma to the Lord; it shall be offered besides the regular burnt offering and its drink offering (Num 28:24).

Some of these offerings were eaten by both the priests and the Jews. Offerings were often cooked and most of it eaten by the offerer, with parts given to the Kohen priests and small parts burned on the altar of the Temple in Jerusalem. In certain special cases, all of the offering was given only to God, such as in the case of the scapegoat.[13] Multiple verses from the Old Testament indicate that the Jews ate the sacrifices:

> Lev 7:19 'The flesh that touches any unclean thing shall not be eaten. It shall be burned with fire. *And as for the clean flesh, all who are clean may eat of it*.

> Lev 7:20 But *the person who eats the flesh of the sacrifice of the peace offering that belongs to the Lord, while he is unclean, that person shall be cut off from his people*.

> Exo 12:6 Now you shall keep it until the fourteenth day of the same month. Then the whole assembly of the congregation of Israel shall kill it at twilight.

> Exo 12:7 And they shall take some of the blood and put it on the two doorposts and on the lintel of the houses where they eat it.

---

[13] Tracey R. Rich, "Qorbanot: Sacrifices and Offerings," *Judaism 101* (1998–2011); Morris Jastrow, et al. "Azazel" Jewish Encyclopedia (1906).

Exo 12:8 Then *they shall eat the flesh on that night; roasted in fire, with unleavened bread and with bitter herbs they shall eat it*.

Exo 12:9 *Do not eat it raw*, nor boiled at all with water, but roasted in fire--its head with its legs and its entrails.

Exo 12:10 *You shall let none of it remain until morning*, and what remains of it until morning you shall burn with fire.

Num 9:9 Then the Lord spoke to Moses, saying,

Num 9:10 "Speak to the children of Israel, saying: 'If anyone of you or your posterity is unclean because of a corpse, or is far away on a journey, he may still keep the Lord's Passover.

Num 9:11 On the fourteenth day of the second month, at twilight, they may keep it. *They shall eat it with unleavened bread and bitter herbs*.

Num 9:12 *They shall leave none of it until morning*, nor break one of its bones. According to all the ordinances of the Passover they shall keep it.

As per these verses, the Jews ate of the sacrifices that they brought to the Lord. Therefore, during the Feast of Unleavened Bread, they would have also partaken in these meals, in addition to eating the unleavened bread that they were commanded to eat. Because the terms "Passover" and "Feast of Unleavened Bread" were used interchangeably at the time of Jesus, John's reference to eating "the Passover" in John 18:28 should be read as eating one of the meals during the week of the Feast of Unleavened Bread.

(b) Trial of Jesus on the Preparation Day of the Passover

John wrote that Pilate came out to the Jews and questioned them and then questioned Jesus, ultimately concluding that he found no fault with Jesus (John 18:29-38), yet the Jews cried out against Jesus (John 19:12). Pilate brought Jesus out and sat down in the judgment seat (John 19:13). He writes, "it was the Preparation Day of the Passover, and about the sixth hour" (John 19:14).[14]

---

[14] The sixth hour could mean noon or midnight, but if John used the supposed Roman time, it would mean 6:00 am or 6:00 pm.

Here, "Preparation Day" refers to the Friday before the Sabbath. On the Preparation Day, Jews prepared for the Sabbath, since they were unable to do any work on the Sabbath. The Preparation Day cannot mean the day prior to Passover (i.e., 13 Nisan) because "Preparation Day" has no such use in the Old or New Testaments. It can therefore only refer to the Preparation Day of the Sabbath. By "Preparation Day of the Passover," John means the Preparation Day of the Sabbath of Passover week (i.e., the Preparation Day of the Sabbath that fell during the week of Passover and the Feast of Unleavened Bread).

(c) Breaking the Legs on the Preparation Day

John wrote that "because it was the <u>Preparation Day</u>, that the bodies should not remain on the cross on the Sabbath (<u>for that Sabbath was a high day</u>), the Jews asked Pilate that their legs might be broken, and that they might be taken away" (John 19:31).

This verse makes clear that the "Preparation Day" referenced in John 19:14 is the Preparation Day of the Sabbath (i.e., Good Friday), not a preparation day for Passover.

The verse further makes clear that the Friday of Jesus's crucifixion was *both* the Preparation Day of the weekly Sabbath as well as a high Sabbath—it was the first day of the Feast of Unleavened Bread, or 15 Nisan. John writes that the "Sabbath was a high day").

E. Discrepancies between Versions of the Bible

1. Overview

Dr. Philips writes (p. 14):

> The Second Edition of the translation of the New Testament (1971) profited from textual and linguistic studies published since the Revised Standard Version New Testament was first issued in 1946.19. Consequently, some previously deleted passages were reinstated, and some accepted passages were deleted. "Two passages, the longer ending of Mark (16.9-20) and the account of the woman caught in adultery (John 7.53-8.11), were restored to the text, separated from it by a blank space and accompanied by informative notes... With new manuscript support, two passages, Luke 22.19b·20 and 24.51b, were restored to the text, and one Passage, Luke 22.43-44, was placed in the footnotes, as was a phrase in Luke 12.39."

Dr. Philips thus states that the Revised Standard Version, Second Edition (RS) (1971) reinstated some previously deleted passages, including:

- The longer ending of Mark (Mark 16:9-20); and
- The account of the woman caught in adultery (John 7:53-8:11), were restored to the text, separated from it by a blank space and accompanied by informative notes...With new manuscript support, two passages, Luke

2. Response

However, both of the referenced passages were included in the RSV of 1952, as well as in the ASV of 1901, on which the 1952 RSV was based. It is therefore inaccurate to state that these passages "were restored to the text."

F. The Early Church Opposed Iconography Because It Is a Form of Idolatry

1. Overview

Dr. Philips writes (p. 71-72):

> Jesus did not condone the pagan practice of making images of God. He upheld the prohibition mentioned in the Torah, Exodus 20 verse 4: "You shall not make for yourself a graven image, or any likeness of anything that is in heaven above, or that is in the earth beneath, or that is in the water under the earth." Consequently, the use of religious images, called icons, was firmly opposed by the early generation of Christian scholars. However, in time, the Greek and Roman tradition of image-making and portraying God in human form eventually won out.

2. Response

There are multiple problems with Dr. Philips' argument:

- He equates the creation of images of God with a violation of Exodus 20:4, though the two are, in fact, distinct;
- He misstates the history of the church, whose early scholars did not in fact oppose the use of religious imagery.

Each of these points is explored in further detail below.

a) Iconography Is Not a Violation of Exodus 20:4

(1) Overview

It is an error to read Exodus 20:4 as condemning iconography. The word פסל (*pecel*) in the original Hebrew of Exodus 20:4 (Strong's number H6459) can be translated as "idol," "image" or "carved image" according to Strong's Concordance. Modern translations have rendered it as "image" (*e.g.*, the NIV) or "carved image" (*e.g.*, the NKJV). However, to translate it as "image" or "carved image" leads to various contradictions. If the original referred to "carved image," then this would lead to a contradiction with the command made just a few chapters later in Exodus 25:18, where God ordered the Israelites to create a graven image of cherubim for the Ark ("make two cherubim of gold, of hammered work you shall make them"). It would also lead to multiple other contradictions in the Bible, including with God's command to "make a snake image and mount it on a pole" in Numbers 21:8.

If the Hebrew word פסל (*pecel*) is translated as "image," we end up with even more contradictions, since the term "image" encompasses both graven (three-dimensional) and non-graven (two-dimensional) images. It would thus encompass the problems noted above with respect to creating graven images and would further lead to issues with two-dimensional images. Unless God would allow His Word to contradict itself, the word פסל in the original Hebrew of Exodus 20:4 cannot be read to mean "image," "carved image" or "graven image." Instead, the word should be translated as "idol," which is one of its alternate meanings.

The fact that פסל (*pecel*) in Exodus 20:4 is intended to mean "idol" is made clear from the following:

(2) Historical Context

God repeatedly berated the Israelites for making and worshipping golden idols. There is no such beratement for merely creating images. On the contrary, God specifically commanded the Israelites to create images to be used *for* worship, as with the hammered golden cherubim in Exodus 25:18, or for miracle working, as with the snake image mounted on a pole in Numbers 21:8, as discussed above. It is only when the Israelites turn to worshipping images that the images become forbidden idols. This was the case, for example, of the Israelites' worship of the bronze serpent in 2 Kings 18. Hezekiah began to reign as king of Judah (2Ki 18:1, 5). Hezekiah is described as a righteous king who "did what was right in the sight of the Lord, according to all that his father David had done" (2Ki 18:3). Among his acts, he "removed the high places and broke the sacred pillars, cut down the wooden image and broke in pieces the bronze serpent that Moses had made; for until those days the children of Israel burned incense to it, and called it Nehushtan" (2Ki 18:4).

(3) Textual Context

The verses following Exodus 20:4 make clear that it is idolatry, not the creation of images, that is forbidden:

> Exo 20:4 "You shall not make for yourself a carved image--any likeness of anything that is in heaven above, or that is in the earth beneath, or that is in the water under the earth;
>
> Exo 20:5 you shall not bow down to them nor serve them. For I, the Lord your God, am a jealous God, visiting the iniquity of the fathers upon the children to the third and fourth generations of those who hate Me,
>
> Exo 20:6 but showing mercy to thousands, to those who love Me and keep My commandments.

Exodus 20:4 should be read in conjunction with Exodus 20:5 such that it is not the creation of images, on its own, that is prohibited. Rather, it is bowing down and worshipping such created images, thereby rendering them into idols, that is forbidden.

b) Early Christian Scholars Did Not Oppose the Use of Religious Images

Dr. Philips gives no support for his contention that icons were "firmly opposed by the early generation of Christian scholars" (p. 71). In fact, icons were used by the early church with little or no objection from its earliest days. According to Professor Michael J. Svigel's paper, "A Few Thoughts on the Tradition of Icons in the Early Church," "[a]lmost all historians of Christianity, however, agree that artwork and symbols have been a part of the Christian tradition from the beginning—whether it be the display of the cross, the symbol of the ICTHUS, or artwork on the walls of catacombs." His paper also states that "[e]arly Christians clearly demonstrate that they viewed artistic expressions as beneficial, as is indicated by the catacomb frescos dating to the second century."

Iconoclasm (icon smashing) came to a head in the eighth century, when the Second Council of Nicaea of 787 (the Seventh Ecumenical Council) determined that icons did not violate the Second Commandment and that they were to be permitted in Orthodox life and worship. Patriarch Paul IV of Constantinople (a former iconoclast) recommended to Empress Irene that she summon an ecumenical council to correct the former iconoclastic views. Iconoclasm was condemned and the use of icons was upheld.

Iconoclasm once again resurfaced in the early ninth century, in 814, in what is the second iconoclast period, after Leo V's accession. The use of icons was forbidden at a council in 815. This second iconoclast period ended with the death of Emperor Theophilus in 842. In 843, his widow restored icon veneration, putting to rest the iconoclasm controversy.

G. Isaiah 42 Prophesies the Coming of Muhammad

1. Overview

Dr. Philips argues that Isaiah prophesies the coming of Muḥammad (p. 75-76):

> In Isaiah 42, Isaiah prophesies about a chosen "Servant of the Lord" whose prophetic mission would be to all mankind, unlike the Hebrew prophets whose missions were limited to Israel. "1 Behold my servant, whom I uphold, my chosen, in whom my soul delights; I have put my Spirit upon him. he will bring forth justice to the nations ... 4 He will not fail or be discouraged till he has established justice in the earth; and the coast lands wait for his law ... 11 Let the desert and its cities lift up their voice, the villages that Kedar inhabits." This particular servant of the Lord is the only one identified with Kedar, the Arabs.

Dr. Philips' argument is not entirely clear, but it appears to be that because Kedar is associated with the Arabs, the prophet identified in Isaiah 42 must be Muḥammad, an Arab, not Jesus, a Jew.

According to the NIV Study Bible footnotes at Isaiah 22:16, Kedar was the "home of Bedouin tribes in the Arabian Desert. Kedar was known for its flocks (60:7; Eze 27:21)."

2. Response

Dr. Philips' argument is flawed in the following ways:

- Using Dr. Philips' logic, Isaiah 42 cannot refer to Muhammad because "Sela" is the naturally fortified capital of the Edomites south of the Dead Sea. The Edomites are the sons of Jacob's brother Esau, who was in turn a son of Isaac, not Ishmael.
- What Isaiah 42:11 is saying is not that God's promised Servant would come from the villages of Kedar or from Sela, but rather, that all peoples, including the Ishmaelites and Edomites, would be able to rejoice at His coming, for He would bring salvation and redemption to all, through grace by faith.

H. Muhammad as the Promised "Comforter" (*Paraklētos*)

1. Dr. Philips' Overall Argument

a) Overview

Dr. Philips writes (p. 73):

> There are also some references in the Gospels which seem to refer to the coming of Prophet Muhammad-may God's peace and blessings be on all the prophets. In the Gospel according to John 14:16, Jesus is quoted as saying, "And I will pray the Father, and he will give you another Counselor, 125 to be with you forever."

b) Response: The Meaning of παράκλητος (Paraklētos) in John 14:16 Is Made Evident by the Verses that Follow

We can determine whether the *paraklētos* as used in John 14:16 is applicable to the Holy Spirit or to Muhammad by examining the verses following John 14:16 in the Gospel of John. These verses make clear that the *paraklētos* is a spirit rather than a physical person.

(1) John 14:17 and John 15:26 Attest that the "Comforter" is a "Spirit"

John 14:17 and John 15:26 make clear that the "comforter" is a "spirit," not a person:

- John 14:17 ("the *Spirit of truth*, whom the world cannot receive, because it neither sees Him nor knows Him; but you know Him, for He dwells with you and will be in you") states that the Comforter is "the Spirit of truth" that the world does not "see," but rather, that "dwells" in Jesus' followers.

- John 15:26 states that the Comforter (here translated as "Helper") is "*the Spirit of truth* who proceeds from the Father."

John 14:17 and 15:26 thus make it clear that the Comforter (Helper, Counselor, etc.) is an unseen spirit. The Comforter therefore cannot be Muhammad, who was a mere man who was seen and composed of flesh and bone.

John 14:17 further makes clear that the *Paraklētos* "dwells with you and will be in you" (John 14:17). This parallels the coming of the Holy Spirit on Pentecost, when the disciples were "all filled with the Holy Spirit" (Acts 2:4). That the Holy Spirit is the John 14:17 *paraklētos* that dwells in us is made clear by Romans 8:9: "you are not in the flesh but in the Spirit, if indeed the Spirit of God dwells in you." Through the Holy Spirit, we are in Jesus, just as Jesus is "in My Father" (John 14:20). None of these words can be said about Muhammad, who does not "dwell" in the people of God as the *paraklētos* (Holy Spirit) does.

(2) John 14:26 Equates the Comforter with the "Holy Spirit"

John 14:26 makes it explicitly clear that the *paraklētos* (translated "Helper" in the NKJV) is the Holy Spirit because it equates the two: "But the Helper [*paraklētos*], the Holy Spirit, whom the Father will send in My name, He will teach you all things." Here, the clause "Holy Spirit" refers back to "Helper," which is the NKJV translation of the Greek παράκλητος (*paraklētos*).

2. The John 16:7 "Comforter" Cannot be the Holy Spirit Because the Comforter Is Yet to Come

a) Overview

Next, Dr. Philips argues that the Comforter (translated "Counselor" in the RSV quoted by Dr. Philips) of John 16:7 cannot be the Holy Spirit because the Comforter is yet to come, but the Holy Spirit had already come (p. 74-75):

> Christian laymen usually interpret the "Counselor" mentioned in John 14:16 as the Holy Spirit. However, the phrase "another Counselor" implies that it will be someone else like Jesus and not the Holy Spirit, especially considering John 16:7, in which Jesus is reported to have said, "Nevertheless I tell you the truth: it is to your advantage that I go away, for if I do not go away, the Counselor will

not come to you, but if I go, I will send him to you." The term "Counselor" could not be referring to the Holy Spirit here, because according to the Gospels, the Holy Spirit was already present in the world prior to Jesus' birth, as well as during his ministry. This verse implies that the "Counselor" had not already come.

Dr. Philips supports his point by pointing to three instances where the Holy Spirit was present in the Gospels prior to Jesus' departure. These instances relate to John the Baptist and his parents, Elizabeth and Zechariah, who were all filled with the Holy Spirit (Footnote 28, p. 74):

> John the Baptist was filled with the Holy Spirit while in his mother's womb (Luke 1:15); Elizabeth was filled with the Holy Spirit (Luke 1:41); John's father, Zacharias, was also filled with the Holy Spirit (Luke 1:67).

Dr. Philips reasons that the Counselor could not have been the Holy Spirit because the Counselor would only come to us if Jesus went away, in accordance with John 16:7.

b) Response

Dr. Philips is correct that the Holy Spirit appeared in the Bible prior to Jesus' departure. In fact, it would be true to state that the Holy Spirit has always been with us, since the beginning of time. The fact that the Holy Spirit manifested Himself in history, including through filling John the Baptist and his parents, Zacharias and Elizabeth, prior to Jesus' departure does not counter Jesus' statement He would send the Holy Spirit after His departure.

When Jesus stated in John 16:7 that "if I do not go away, the Helper will not come to you; but if I depart, I will send Him to you," He was addressing the twelve Apostles at the Last Supper. He was not addressing John the Baptist or his parents, Zacharias and Elizabeth. Therefore, it is not relevant that John, Zacharias and Elizabeth were previously filled with the Holy Spirit. What is relevant is that the audience that Jesus was addressing—namely, the 12 Apostles—had not yet been filled with the Holy Spirit. This infilling had not happened until the Holy Spirit descended upon the Apostles 50 days after the resurrection, on Pentecost.

Therefore, when Jesus promised in John 16:17 that He would send the Holy Spirit to the Apostles, He was referring to Pentecost, when the Holy Spirit filled the Apostles who were gathered together (Acts 2:1-4).

Pentecost was thus the fulfillment of Jesus' promise to send the "Counselor" or "Comforter" (*paraklētos*) to the Apostles during the Last Supper in John 16:7.

Chapter 4. Claim That Paul Changed Jesus' Gospel and Practices

A. Overview of Dr. Philips' Claim

Dr. Philips writes (p. 78):

> about five years after the end of Jesus' ministry, a young rabbi by the name of Saul of Tarsus, who claimed to have seen Jesus in a vision, began to change Jesus' way. Paul (his Roman name) had considerable respect for Roman philosophy and he spoke proudly of his own Roman citizenship. His conviction was that non-Jews who became Christians should not be burdened with the Torah in any respect. The author of Acts 13:39 quotes Paul as saying, "And by him every one that believes is freed from everything from which you could not be freed by the law of Moses." It was primarily through the efforts of Paul that the Church began to take on its non-Jewish character. Paul wrote most of the New Testament letters (epistles), which the Church accepts as the official doctrine and inspired Scripture. These letters do not preserve the Gospel of Jesus or even represent it; instead, Paul transformed the teachings of Christ into a Hellenic (Graeco-Roman) philosophy.

Dr. Philips then goes on to argue that Paul abolished the institution of circumcision, the prohibition on consuming pork and alcohol, ritual slaughter so as to drain animals of blood prior to consumption, ablution before prayer, prostration in prayer, veiling, the greeting "peace be with you," fasting, prohibitions on interest and the institution of polygamy. We examine each of these institutions in turn.

B. General Response: Christians are No Longer Bound by the Old Testament Law

1. The Purpose of the Old Testament Law Was to Convict Us of Sin

God revealed the Mosaic Law in order to convict the Jews of sin. However, the Mosaic Law cannot justify a person.[15] The law serves to bring knowledge of sin, but it does not justify because all have broken the law "and fall short of the glory of God" (Rom 3:23).

2. Jesus Fulfilled the Letter of the Law

Jesus stated that "till heaven and earth pass away, one jot or one tittle will by no means pass from the law till all is fulfilled" (Mat 5:18). But Jesus also declared that He was the fulfillment of the law: "Do not think that I came to destroy the Law or the Prophets. I did not come to destroy but to fulfill" (Mat 5:17). Jesus was the fulfillment of this law. He was sent by God to fulfill the law by acting as a sacrifice to atone for sin once and for all.

In this light, the Apostle Paul wrote that "when we were in the flesh, the sinful passions which were aroused by the law were at work in our members to bear fruit to death. But now we have been delivered from the law, having died to what we were held by, so that we should serve in the newness of the Spirit and not in the oldness of the letter" (Rom 7:5-6). Deliverance from the law was achieved by Jesus, who saved us from the bondage of the law, which "was our tutor to bring us to Christ, that we might be justified by faith. But after faith has come, we are no longer under a tutor" (Gal 3:24-25).

Through faith, everyone who believes in Jesus is justified. Paul writes that "a man is justified by faith apart from the deeds of the law" (Rom 3:28). "[E]veryone who believes is justified from all things from which you could not be justified by the law of Moses" (Acts 13:39) and is "justified freely by His grace through the redemption that is in Christ Jesus" (Rom 3:24).

3. The Council of Jerusalem Subjects Christians to Four Prohibitions (Idols, Blood, Things Strangled, Sexual Immorality); Other Than This, Christians are Bound by the Spirit of the Law: To Love One's Neighbor

---

[15] Rom 3:20 ("by the deeds of the law no flesh will be justified in His sight, for by the law is the knowledge of sin").

a)   Council of Jerusalem

The Council of Jerusalem or Apostolic Council was held in Jerusalem around AD 50. The Council decided that Gentile converts to Christianity were not obligated to keep most of the Law of Moses, including requirement of circumcision. The Council did, however, retain the prohibitions on idols, blood, strangled animals and sexual immorality. These prohibitions are sometimes referred to as the Apostolic Decree or Jerusalem Quadrilateral.

The council is recounted in Acts 15:

> Acts 15:28 For it seemed good to the Holy Spirit, and to us, to lay upon you no greater burden than these necessary things:

> Acts 15:29 that you abstain from things offered to idols, from blood, from things strangled, and from sexual immorality. If you keep yourselves from these, you will do well. Farewell.

b)   The Spirit of the Law: To Love One's Neighbor

Other than the Jerusalem Quadrilateral, Christians are bound by the spirit of the law: to love God and love one's neighbor as oneself. "For all the law is fulfilled in one word, even in this: 'YOU SHALL LOVE YOUR NEIGHBOR AS YOURSELF'" (Gal 5:14). Jesus emphasized this in His teachings. When a lawyer asked him, "which is the great commandment in the law?" (Mat 22:36), He replied:

> Mat 22:37 'YOU SHALL LOVE THE Lord YOUR GOD WITH ALL YOUR HEART, WITH ALL YOUR SOUL, AND WITH ALL YOUR MIND.'

> Mat 22:38 This is the first and great commandment.

> Mat 22:39 And the second is like it: 'YOU SHALL LOVE YOUR NEIGHBOR AS YOURSELF.'

> Mat 22:40 On these two commandments hang all the Law and the Prophets.

c)   The Spirit Leads to Good Works and Salvation

When one is filled with the Spirit, his life becomes characterized by good works and a cessation of sin. One ceases engaging in idolatry, adultery, drunkenness and other sins. Paul makes this clear in 1 Corinthians:

1Co 6:9 Do you not know that the unrighteous will not inherit the kingdom of God? Do not be deceived. Neither fornicators, nor idolaters, nor adulterers, nor homosexuals, nor sodomites,

1Co 6:10 nor thieves, nor covetous, nor drunkards, nor revilers, nor extortioners will inherit the kingdom of God.

1Co 6:11 And such were some of you. But you were washed, but you were sanctified, but you were justified in the name of the Lord Jesus and by the Spirit of our God.

Paul goes on to list the works of the flesh and contrast them with the fruit of the Spirit in Galatians:

Gal 5:19 Now the works of the flesh are evident, which are: adultery, fornication, uncleanness, lewdness,

Gal 5:20 idolatry, sorcery, hatred, contentions, jealousies, outbursts of wrath, selfish ambitions, dissensions, heresies,

Gal 5:21 envy, murders, drunkenness, revelries, and the like; of which I tell you beforehand, just as I also told you in time past, that those who practice such things will not inherit the kingdom of God.

Gal 5:22 But the fruit of the Spirit is love, joy, peace, longsuffering, kindness, goodness, faithfulness,

Gal 5:23 gentleness, self-control. Against such there is no law.

Gal 5:24 And those who are Christ's have crucified the flesh with its passions and desires.

If a person is filled with the Spirit, his life will be reflected by its fruit, not because the person strives to obey the Old Testament Law, but because the Spirit of God dwells in him.

4.   The Spirit of the Law Requires a Higher Standard

Jesus taught in the Sermon on the Mount that His followers are called to a standard that is higher than that established in the letter of the law.

For example, Jesus teaches that it is not enough to obey the commandment not to murder. Christians must go further than this and not even get angry with their brothers without a cause or call their brothers "Raca" (foolish):

Mat 5:21 "You have heard that it was said to those of old, 'YOU SHALL NOT MURDER, and whoever murders will be in danger of the judgment.'

Mat 5:22 But I say to you that whoever is angry with his brother without a cause shall be in danger of the judgment. And whoever says to his brother, 'Raca!' shall be in danger of the council. But whoever says, 'You fool!' shall be in danger of hell fire.

Similarly, it is not enough merely to not commit adultery. Christians must go further than this and not even lust after women:

Mat 5:27 "You have heard that it was said to those of old, 'YOU SHALL NOT COMMIT ADULTERY.'

Mat 5:28 But I say to you that whoever looks at a woman to lust for her has already committed adultery with her in his heart.

Mat 5:29 If your right eye causes you to sin, pluck it out and cast it from you; for it is more profitable for you that one of your members perish, than for your whole body to be cast into hell.

While the Mosaic law permits divorce, Christians must not divorce except for sexual immorality. In other words, even that which is permitted in the Mosaic law is prohibited for Christians, who are called to a higher standard:

Mat 5:31 "Furthermore it has been said, 'Whoever divorces his wife, let him give her a certificate of divorce.'

Mat 5:32 But I say to you that whoever divorces his wife for any reason except sexual immorality causes her to commit adultery; and whoever marries a woman who is divorced commits adultery.

Similarly, it is not enough to merely refrain from swearing falsely. Jesus calls Christians to a higher standard, prohibiting His followers from swearing at all:

Mat 5:33 "Again you have heard that it was said to those of old, 'You shall not swear falsely, but shall perform your oaths to the Lord.'

Mat 5:34 But I say to you, do not swear at all: neither by heaven, for it is God's throne;

Mat 5:35 nor by the earth, for it is His footstool; nor by Jerusalem, for it is the city of the great King.

Mat 5:36 Nor shall you swear by your head, because you cannot make one hair white or black.

Mat 5:37 But let your 'Yes' be 'Yes,' and your 'No,' 'No.' For whatever is more than these is from the evil one.

5. Christians Follow the Law of Grace

Through Jesus' sacrifice, Christians are no longer bound by the Mosaic Law; they are now governed by the law of grace. The "law was given through Moses, but grace and truth came through Jesus Christ" (John 1:17).

6. Responding to Dr. Philips Requires Distinguishing Mosaic Ceremonial Laws, Civil Laws and Moral Laws[16]

The Old Testament laws fall into three categories:
-   Civil Laws governed the nation of Israel, encompassing behavior and defining punishments for crimes.
-   Ceremonial Laws governed "clean" and "unclean" things, various kinds of sacrifices and temple practices.
-   Moral Laws declared God's will as to right and wrong. It includes, for example, the 10 Commandments.

a) Civil Laws

These laws overlapped in biblical Israel, which was a unique society in that it was established as a nation governed by God. Unlike modern polities, where states are governed by secular laws passed by representative majorities, biblical Israel was governed by biblical law, not the democratic will. There was no separation of church and state. Israel's biblical civil laws are not relevant to or binding upon modern secular states because God no longer has a nation-state on earth; His Kingdom is not of this world. However, principles of biblical Israel (e.g., regarding hygiene, caring for the poor, health, etc.) can guide us on best practices.

---

[16] *See* "Why Don't We Follow All of the Old Testament Laws?" available at <https://jdgreear.com/blog/why-dont-we-follow-all-of-the-old-testament-laws/> for a fuller discussion.

b) Ceremonial Laws

The Ceremonial Laws illustrate for us God's holiness as contrasted by our unholiness. The purpose of the sacrificial system was to highlight the deep chasm between our sins and God's sinlessness. These sacrifices were fulfilled in Jesus' crucifixion on Passover. Jesus' sacrifices fulfilled the Old Testament sacrifices once and for all. To continue the Old Testament sacrifices as atonement for our sins would negate the ultimate atonement that God made.

c) Moral Laws

Jesus fulfilled the moral laws through His perfect living, but unlike the civil and ceremonial laws, which were given to a particular people in a particular historical context, the moral laws are timeless. When Jesus mentioned the moral laws, he reaffirmed them or raised them to a higher standard.

Today, Christians are to keep the moral law not as a means of earning salvation—their salvation was already purchased through the blood of Jesus. Rather, they keep the moral law out of a deep and abiding love for God. Loving God means loving what God loves, including justice and mercy, and therefore keeping the moral law.

7. While Christians Are No Longer Bound by the Mosaic Law, Many Continue to Observe It for Health Rather than Religious Reasons

Western societies that observe Mosaic legal principles, including practicing circumcision and refraining from consuming pork and blood, do so for health rather than religious reasons. For example, studies have shown that circumcision leads to a decrease in disease, that pork may have adverse health effects given its high cholesterol and saturated fat and that blood carries toxins. Many western nations having a Judeo-Christian heritage therefore continue to practice circumcision and refrain from pork and blood.

The origins of these practices are religious. For example, the prohibition on consuming blood derives from the role of blood in making atonement for sin:

> Lev 17:11 For the life of the flesh is in the blood, and I have given it to you upon the altar to make atonement for your souls; for it is the blood that makes atonement for the soul.'

Lev 17:12 Therefore I said to the children of Israel, 'No one among you shall eat blood, nor shall any stranger who dwells among you eat blood.'

However, in the West, refraining from consuming blood is not based on religious practice. Rather, it is based on scientific understanding that blood carries disease and toxins. We have modern science that teaches us the benefits of the Mosaic legal practices that were given to Israel millennia ago. We do not practice them out of a sense of good works for salvation; Jesus already earned our salvation. Rather, we practice them as good practices to promote health.

C. Specific Claims and Responses

1. Circumcision

a) Overview

(1) Circumcision

Dr. Philips points out that in Genesis 17:10-13, God commanded circumcision of the Israelites. In Luke 2:21, Jesus was circumcised when he was eight days old. "Consequently, to be circumcised was part of Jesus' way" (p. 80). However, Paul changed this practice (p. 80):

> He claimed that circumcision was the circumcision of the heart. In his letter to the Romans 2:29, he wrote: "He is a Jew who is one inwardly, and real circumcision is a matter of the heart, spiritual and not literal." In his letter to the Galatians 5:2, he wrote: "Now I, Paul, say to you that if you receive circumcision, Christ will be of no advantage to you." This was Paul's false interpretation. On the other hand, Jesus was not circumcised in the heart nor did he say anything about circumcision of the heart; he kept the "everlasting covenant" and was circumcised in the flesh. Thus, an important part of following the way of Jesus is circumcision.

b) Response

(1) Circumcision Is Not Part of Jesus' "Way" Because He Was Not of the Age of Reason When He Was Circumcised

Yet even if Jesus' circumcision should be viewed as part of "Jesus' way," as Dr. Philips argued, and therefore binding on Christians, we must remember that Jesus was circumcised before He was of the age of reason. The fact that Jesus was circumcised when he was eight days old is not evidence that circumcision was part of His "way" or that His actions implied that His followers were bound by Mosaic ceremonial laws. He was not of an age to make a conscious decision when He was circumcised. The decision to circumcise Him was taken by His parents. To accept Dr. Philips' argument would be the equivalent of saying that whatever decision that Jesus' parents took for him while He was an infant are part of Jesus' way and are therefore binding upon all generations of later Christians. Such an argument ignores the role of conscious reasoning and its absence in infancy.

2. Pork

a) *Overview*

Dr. Philips writes (p. 81):

> Jesus did not eat pork. He followed the laws of Moses and he did not eat pork. In Leviticus 11:7-8, "7 And the swine, because it parts the hoof and is cloven-footed but does not chew the cud, is unclean to you. 8 their flesh you shall not eat, and their carcasses you shall not touch; they are unclean to you." Jesus' only dealing with pigs was his permission to the unclean spirits which were possessing a man to enter them. When they entered the herd of pigs, they ran into the water and drowned. However, most people who call themselves Christians today not only eat pork, they love it so much that they have made pigs the subject of nursery rhymes [e.g. This little piggy went to market...] and children's stories [e.g. The Three Little Pigs]. Porky Pig is a very popular cartoon character and recently a full-length feature movie was made about a pig called "Babe". Thus, it may be said that those who call themselves followers of Christ are not in fact following the way of Christ.

b) *Response*

(1) We Do Not Have a Complete Record of Jesus' Diet; He Could Have Eaten Forbidden Foods If It Was to Protect Life

We do not have a complete historical record of what Jesus ate. The Gospels record that He ate bread and fish, but they do not provide a comprehensive account of everything else that He ate or refrained from eating.

It is possible that Jesus would have eaten pork or other forbidden foods if it was a matter of life and death because He taught that the purpose of the law was to preserve life. The Gospels teach (Mark 2:23-28):

> Now it happened that He went through the grainfields on the Sabbath; and as they went His disciples began to pluck the heads of grain.

> And the Pharisees said to Him, "Look, why do they do what is not lawful on the Sabbath?"

> But He said to them, "Have you never read what David did when he was in need and hungry, he and those with him:

> how he went into the house of God in the days of Abiathar the high priest, and ate the showbread, which is not lawful to eat except for the priests, and also gave some to those who were with him?"

> And He said to them, "The Sabbath was made for man, and not man for the Sabbath.

> Therefore, the Son of Man is also Lord of the Sabbath."

While there is no record of Jesus consuming pork or blood, it is conceivable that He would have allowed it because He emphasized following the spirit of the law, which is to promote life.

(2) Christians Were Set Free from Old Testament Dietary Laws

That Christians were set free from Old Testament dietary laws was made clear to the vision given to Peter in Acts. As Peter went up to a roof to pray, he fell into a trance and saw heaven open and a great sheet descending down to him (Acts 10:9-11). In it were four-footed animals, creeping things and birds (Acts 10:12) and a voice commanded him to kill and eat (Acts 10:13). Peter protested, saying that he had never eaten anything common or unclean (Acts 10:14). The voice said that he must not call common what God has cleansed (Acts 10:15). This happened three times (Acts 10:16).

3. Ritual Slaughter to Drain Animals of Blood

a) Overview

Dr. Philips writes (p. 82-83):

> Jesus also did not eat anything containing blood, nor did he eat blood. God is recorded as having instructed Prophet Moses in the Torah, Deuteronomy 12:16, "Only you shall not eat the blood; you shall pour it upon the earth like water," and in Leviticus 19:26, "You shall not eat any flesh with the blood in it. You shall not practice augury or witchcraft" …

> Jesus and his early followers observed the proper method of slaughter by mentioning God's name and cutting the jugular veins of the animals while they were living to allow the heart to pump out the blood. However, Christians today do not attach much importance to proper slaughter methods, as prescribed by God.

b) Response

(1) Christians Maintain the Old Testament Prohibition on Consuming Blood

The Council of Jerusalem or Apostolic Council decided that Gentile converts to Christianity were not obligated to keep most of the Law of Moses. The Council did, however, retain the prohibitions on idols, blood, strangled animals and sexual immorality. These prohibitions are sometimes referred to as the Apostolic Decree or Jerusalem Quadrilateral.

The Council is recounted in Acts 15:

> Acts 15:28 For it seemed good to the Holy Spirit, and to us, to lay upon you no greater burden than these necessary things:

> Acts 15:29 that you abstain from things offered to idols, from blood, from things strangled, and from sexual immorality. If you keep yourselves from these, you will do well. Farewell.

Christians therefore maintain the Old Testament prohibition on consuming blood. As discussed below, slaughter in many countries, particularly in the West, is designed in a way that allows the blood to be drained. This is followed mainly out of a sense of health and hygiene rather than religious doctrine, though Judeo-Christian prohibitions on consuming blood likely play a role.

(2) Slaughter in the West Follows the Principle that Blood Should Be Drained

As an example of practices of western societies that follow Mosaic legal principles out of a sense of health rather than out of a sense of religious obligation, we can consider the slaughter of livestock in the United States, which follows the principle of the Mosaic law about not consuming blood, though it does not follow the letter of the oral tradition establishing kosher slaughter techniques.

The Mosaic law commands:

> Deu 12:16 Only you shall not eat the blood; you shall pour it on the earth like water.

> Lev 19:26 'You shall not eat anything with the blood, nor shall you practice divination or soothsaying.'

The Israelites accordingly developed kosher slaughter techniques to ensure that blood was drained. These specific methods were not prescribed in the written law given to Moses[17]:

> The laws regarding the precise method of slaughter are not stated in the Bible, but were given orally to Moses on Mount Sinai, as indicated in the verse by the statement, "as I have commanded thee," that is, as I have already instructed you. [The function of this previous sentence is to make a link between rabbinically developed laws regarding implementation of these laws and what is traditionally understood as the revelation—of both oral and written Torah (which can be translated as both "teaching" and "law")—at Sinai.]

Slaughterhouses in the United States follow the principle of blood draining by hanging animals upside-down and then slitting their throats to allow all of the blood to drain. The process begins with stunning the animal to make the slaughter as painless as possible and then suspending it by a hind limb. They are then typically bled by the insertion of a knife into the thoracic cavity and severance of the carotid artery and jugular vein to allow for the maximum amount of blood removal from the body. The skin is then removed, followed by the removal of the head. The

---

[17] Rabbi Gersion Appel, "Kosher Slaughter: An Introduction," *My Jewish Learning* <https://www.myjewishlearning.com/article/kosher-slaughtering-an-introduction>.

animal is then split and eviscerated. Meat is separated from bones and fat and is then cooled.[18]

4. Prohibition on Consuming Alcohol

a) Overview

Dr. Philips writes (p. 83-84):

> Jesus consecrated himself to God and therefore abstained from alcoholic drinks according to the instructions recorded in Numbers 6:1-4: "And the Lord said to Moses, 2 'Say to the people of Israel, When either a man or a woman makes a special vow, the vow of the Nazirite, 144 to separate himself to the Lord, 3he shall separate himself from wine and strong drink; he shall drink no vinegar made from wine or strong drink, and shall not drink any juice of grapes or eat grapes, fresh or dried. All the days of his separation he shall eat nothing that is produced by the grapevine, not even the seeds or the skins."

b) Response

(1) Jesus Did Not Take a Nazarite Vow

Dr. Philips misunderstands what the Nazarite vow is. When a person takes a Nazarite vow, he refrains from grapes and alcohol, does not shave his hair and does not go near dead bodies (Num 6:3-8):

> Num 6:3 he shall separate himself from wine and similar drink; he shall drink neither vinegar made from wine nor vinegar made from similar drink; neither shall he drink any grape juice, nor eat fresh grapes or raisins.

> Num 6:4 All the days of his separation he shall eat nothing that is produced by the grapevine, from seed to skin.

> Num 6:5 'All the days of the vow of his separation no razor shall come upon his head; until the days are fulfilled for which he separated himself to the Lord, he shall be holy. Then he shall let the locks of the hair of his head grow.

---

[18] See "Livestock Slaughter Procedures," *Encyclopedia Britannica* <https://www.britannica.com/technology/meat-processing/Livestock-slaughter-procedures>.

Num 6:6 All the days that he separates himself to the Lord he shall not go near a dead body.

Num 6:7 He shall not make himself unclean even for his father or his mother, for his brother or his sister, when they die, because his separation to God is on his head.

Num 6:8 All the days of his separation he shall be holy to the Lord.

Dr. Philips offers no evidence whatsoever that Jesus ever took such a vow. Dr. Philips states that Jesus "consecrated himself to God" (p. 83) and misleadingly equates such consecration to the taking up of a Nazarite vow, as though every man who ever consecrates himself to God is prohibited from eating grapes, drinking wine, cutting his hair or approaching dead bodies.

There is nothing in the Gospels that suggests that Jesus ever took a Nazarite vow. On the contrary, a holistic reading of the Gospels makes clear that Jesus never took such a vow. If Jesus took a Nazarite vow, He would be prohibited from approaching dead bodies, but the Gospels record Jesus not only approaching the dead, but also raising the dead back to life (*see, e.g.,* John 11:1–44, where Jesus brings Lazarus back to life four days after his burial, and Mark 5:21-43, where Jesus raises Jairus's daughter from the dead).

(2) The Gospels Suggest that Jesus Drank Alcohol

Various versus from the New Testament strongly suggest that Jesus drank wine. These include:

- Mat 11:18-19: "For John came neither eating nor drinking, and they say, 'He has a demon.' The Son of Man came eating and drinking, and they say, 'Look, a glutton and a winebibber, a friend of tax collectors and sinners!'" (see also Luke 7:33-34).
- John 2:1-11: Jesus converted water into wine at the wedding in Cana. It is unlikely that Jesus would have done this if He abstained from drinking wine and considered the consumption of wine to be a sin.[19]

---

[19] Dr. Philips challenges the veracity of the account of Jesus' turning water into wine because the miracle "is found only in the Gospel of John, which consistently contradicts the other three gospels. As mentioned earlier, the Gospel of John was opposed as heretical in the early Church" (p. 84). Dr. Philips cites to *The Five Gospels*, p. 20 to support his argument that the Gospel

- Mat 26:27-28: At the last supper, "Jesus took the cup, and gave thanks, and gave it to them, saying, "Drink from it, all of you. Mat 26:28 For this is My blood of the new covenant, which is shed for many for the remission of sins." The cup was most likely wine, because drinking wine was traditionally part of the Passover, where Jews typically drink from four cups of wine.[20]

(3) Wine Was an Important Part of the Hebrew Ceremonial Tradition that Jesus Would Have Taken part In

---

of John was opposed as heretical in the early Church. *The Five Gospels* states "The Fourth Gospel was opposed as heretical in the early Church, and it knows none of the stories associated with John son of Zebedee. In the judgment of many scholars, it was produced by a 'school' of disciples, probably in Syria" (p.20).
The account of *The Five Gospels* is problematic on several levels. First, it offers no citation to bolster its claim that the Fourth Gospel was opposed as heretical in the early Church. Second, it was published by a group of postmodern, theological liberals of The Jesus Seminar, started in 1985 by the late Robert Funk. The fifth Gospel is the Gospel of Thomas, which has strong Gnostic leanings. Third, in concluding that Eighty-two percent of the words ascribed to Jesus in the gospels were not actually spoken by him" (p. 5), the Fellows of the Jesus Seminar used a voting system rather than scientific criteria to determine which words were authentic. According to the Westar Institute:
   After debate on each agenda item, Fellows voted using colored beads to indicate the degree of authenticity of Jesus' words. Each color was assigned a number rating, so that votes could be quantified with a weighted average.
   The Fellows adopted four categories:
   Red (likely authentic)
   Pink (somewhat likely)
   Gray (somewhat unlikely)
   Black (unlikely) [Sayings of Jesus, Jesus Seminar, Westar Institute]
The conclusions of the Jesus Seminar contradict those of other sources. James Malcolm, for example, draws from a wide range of early church fathers who were "unanimous that John wrote the fourth Gospel, and it was authoritative for them" (see https://drjamesmalcolm.wordpress.com/2019/04/15/4-church-fathers-and-johns-gospel).
[20] Naftali Silberberg, "Why four cups of wine by the seder?" <https://www.chabad.org/holidays/passover/pesach_cdo/aid/658549/jewish/Why-four-cups-of-wine.htm>.

The Old Testament has many references to wine. Those that are presented in a negative light (*e.g.*, in the case of Noah and, later, Lot) involve drunkenness, which is clearly prohibited. But those that do not involve drunkenness are not presented in a negative light. In many cases, they are presented as part of Jewish ritual and tradition:

- Gen 14:18-19: "Then Melchizedek king of Salem brought out bread and wine; he was the priest of God Most High. And he blessed him and said: "Blessed be Abram of God Most High, Possessor of heaven and earth.""

- God's ceremonial law requires the use of wine. By way of example only (there are many more references that are not cited herein), we may point to the following:
  - o Exo 29:39-40: "One lamb you shall offer in the morning, and the other lamb you shall offer at twilight. With the one lamb shall be one-tenth of an ephah of flour mixed with one-fourth of a hin of pressed oil, and one-fourth of a hin of wine as a drink offering."
  - o Lev 23:13: "Its grain offering shall be two-tenths of an ephah of fine flour mixed with oil, an offering made by fire to the Lord, for a sweet aroma; and its drink offering shall be of wine, one-fourth of a hin."
  - o Num 15:4-5: "then he who presents his offering to the Lord shall bring a grain offering of one-tenth of an ephah of fine flour mixed with one-fourth of a hin of oil; and one-fourth of a hin of wine as a drink offering you shall prepare with the burnt offering or the sacrifice, for each lamb."
  - o Num 15:7: "as a drink offering you shall offer one-third of a hin of wine as a sweet aroma to the Lord."
  - o Num 15:10: "you shall bring as the drink offering half a hin of wine as an offering made by fire, a sweet aroma to the Lord."
  - o Num 28:14: "Their drink offering shall be half a hin of wine for a bull, one-third of a hin for a ram, and one-fourth of a hin for a lamb; this is the burnt offering for each month throughout the months of the year."
  - o Deu 14:23: "And you shall eat before the Lord your God, in the place where He chooses to make His name abide, the tithe of your grain and your new wine and your oil, of the firstborn

of your herds and your flocks, that you may learn to fear the Lord your God always."

o   Deu 14:24-26: "But if the journey is too long for you, so that you are not able to carry the tithe, or if the place where the Lord your God chooses to put His name is too far from you, when the Lord your God has blessed you, then you shall exchange it for money, take the money in your hand, and go to the place which the Lord your God chooses. And you shall spend that money for whatever your heart desires: for oxen or sheep, for wine or similar drink, for whatever your heart desires; you shall eat there before the Lord your God, and you shall rejoice, you and your household."

There is a strict prohibition on the consumption of wine, but it only involves those who go into the tabernacle of meeting:

Lev 10:9: "Do not drink wine or intoxicating drink, you, nor your sons with you, when you go into the tabernacle of meeting, lest you die. It shall be a statute forever throughout your generations."

Outside of this exception, there is no strict prohibition on drinking alcohol, provided it does not lead to drunkenness.

5.   Ablution before Prayer

a) *Overview*

Dr. Philips writes (p. 84-85):

Prior to making formal prayer, Jesus used to wash his limbs according to the teachings of the Torah. Moses and Aaron are recorded as doing the same in Exodus 40:30-1, "30 And he set the laver between the tent of meeting and the altar, and put water in it for washing, 31 ·with which Moses and Aaron and his sons washed their hands and their feet .... as the Lord commanded Moses."

b) *Response*

Exodus 30 sets forth rules of ritual washing or ablution:

Exo 30:18 "You shall also make a laver of bronze, with its base also of bronze, for washing. You shall put it between the tabernacle of meeting and the altar. And you shall put water in it,

Exo 30:19 for Aaron and his sons shall wash their hands and their feet in water from it.

Exo 30:20 When they go into the tabernacle of meeting, or when they come near the altar to minister, to burn an offering made by fire to the Lord, they shall wash with water, lest they die.

Exo 30:21 So they shall wash their hands and their feet, lest they die. And it shall be a statute forever to them--to him and his descendants throughout their generations."

God commands ritual washing in Exodus 40:

Exo 40:11 And you shall anoint the laver and its base, and consecrate it.

Exo 40:12 "Then you shall bring Aaron and his sons to the door of the tabernacle of meeting and wash them with water.

Exo 40:13 You shall put the holy garments on Aaron, and anoint him and consecrate him, that he may minister to Me as priest.

Exo 40:14 And you shall bring his sons and clothe them with tunics.

Exo 40:15 You shall anoint them, as you anointed their father, that they may minister to Me as priests; for their anointing shall surely be an everlasting priesthood throughout their generations."

Exodus 40-30-32 states the following of Moses:

Exo 40:30 He set the laver between the tabernacle of meeting and the altar, and put water there for washing;

Exo 40:31 and Moses, Aaron, and his sons would wash their hands and their feet with water from it.

Exo 40:32 Whenever they went into the tabernacle of meeting, and when they came near the altar, they washed, as the Lord had commanded Moses.

Ritual washing, or ablution, is one more element of the myriad laws commanded in the Old Testament that Jesus fulfilled and that are no longer applicable to members of the new covenant. The Council of Jerusalem decided that Gentile converts to Christianity were not obligated to keep most of the law of Moses, including ablution laws. The Council retained only the prohibitions on idols, blood, strangled animals and sexual immorality (Acts 15:28-29). These prohibitions are sometimes referred to as the Apostolic Decree or Jerusalem Quadrilateral.

Other than the Jerusalem Quadrilateral, Christians are bound by the spirit of the law: to love God and love one's neighbor as oneself. "For all the law is fulfilled in one word, even in this: 'YOU SHALL LOVE YOUR NEIGHBOR AS YOURSELF'" (Gal 5:14).

In resurrecting Old Testament laws relating to ablution and other practices that were applicable to ancient Israel, Dr. Philips negates the sacrifice that Jesus made on the cross to free Christians of the law and bring forgiveness of their sins.

6. Prostration in Prayer

a) Overview

Dr. Philips writes (p. 85-86):

> Jesus is described in the Gospels as prostrating during prayer. In Matthew 26:39, the author describes an incident which took place when Jesus went with his disciples to Gethsemane: "And going a little farther *he fell on his face and prayed*. 'My Father, if it be possible, let this cup pass from me; nevertheless, not as I will, but as thou wilt."

> Christians today kneel down, clasping their hands, in a posture which cannot be ascribed to Jesus. The method of prostration in prayer followed by Jesus was not of his own making. It was the mode of prayer of the prophets before him. In the Old Testament, Genesis 17:3, Prophet Abraham is recorded to *have fallen on his face in prayer*; in Numbers 16:22 & 20:6, both Moses and Aaron are recorded to have fallen on their faces in worship; in Joshua 5:14 & 7:6, Joshua fell on his face to the earth and worshipped; in I Kings 18:42, Elijah bowed down on the ground and put his face between his knees. This was the way of the prophets through whom God chose to convey His word to the world; and it is only by this way that those who claim to follow Jesus will gain the salvation which he preached in his Gospel.

> Chapter al-Insaan (76):25-6, is only one of many Qur'aanic examples of God's instructions to the believers to bow down in worship to Him.

b) Response

This passage is flawed on multiple levels:

(1) God's Law Does Not Prescribe Prostration

Dr. Philips fails to provide any support whatsoever that prostration in prayer was ever required in the Mosaic law or in ancient Israel's practice, nor does he offer any scriptural support for his assertion that prostration in prayer is the only way "that those who claim to follow Jesus will gain the salvation which he preached in his Gospel" (p. 86).

(2) Christians May Prostrate Themselves in Prayer, and They Often Do

Christians very often kneel down or prostrate themselves in prayer. Eastern Orthodox priests prostrate themselves before the Eucharist during liturgy. The Orthodox kneel during the sacrament of confession. Catholic churches typically have kneelers for parishioners to use during worship. Protestants often have altar calls where worshippers bow down at the altar in prayer and worship. In addition, Christians spontaneously kneel or prostrate themselves in worship.

(3) The Passages Cited by Dr. Philips Are Spontaneous Instances of Prostration, Not Instances of Following Prescribed Rituals or Laws

The passages cited are of instances in which Jesus, Abraham, Moses, Aaron, Joshua and Elijah spontaneously fell down in prayer. They are *not* instances where they were following a prescribed ritual. Rather, they relate to instances in which individuals, overwhelmed with emotion or with the presence of God, spontaneously prostrated themselves.

(4) Jesus Taught That It Is the Condition of Heart that Counts, Not Physical Movements

Jesus does not prescribe ritualistic prayer. He warned against ostentatious displays in prayer:

> Mat 6:5 "And when you pray, you shall not be like the hypocrites. For they love to pray standing in the synagogues and on the corners of the streets, that they may be seen by men. Assuredly, I say to you, they have their reward.

> Mat 6:6 But you, when you pray, go into your room, and when you have shut your door, pray to your Father who is in the secret place; and your Father who sees in secret will reward you openly.

He warned against empty ritual and "vain repetition" in prayer. He taught: "when you pray, do not use vain repetitions as the heathen do. For they think that they will be heard for their many words" (Mat 6:7).

Instead, He taught His followers to address God as "Father" and prescribed a conversational prayer (Mat 6:9-13; Luke 11:1-28).

7. Veiling

Dr. Philips writes that God's law required that women cover their hair with a veil and this practice is reflected in the Old Testament and is commanded by Paul in the New Testament. However, today's Christians have discontinued the practice, whereas Muslims continue it. The following sections will examine each of Dr. Philips' arguments in turn.

a) Cultural Practice

(1) Overview

Dr. Philips writes (p. 86):

> The women around Jesus veiled themselves according to the practice of the women around the earlier prophets. Their garments were loose and covered their bodies completely, and they wore scarves which covered their hair.

(2) Response

Dr. Philips offers no evidence whatsoever to support his claims. In fact, we will likely never know whether women around Jesus wore loose garments and "covered their bodies completely" and covered their hair. Yet even if this did, this would constitute cultural tradition. The Mosaic law did not command that women cover their bodies completely with loose garments or that they cover their hair.

b) Rebekah Covered Herself

(1) Overview

Dr. Philips writes (p. 86):

In Genesis 24:64-5: "And Rebekah lifted up her eyes, and when she saw Isaac, she alighted from the camel, 65 and said to the servant, 'Who is the man yonder, walking in the field to meet us?' The servant said, 'It is my master.' So she took her veil and covered herself."

(2) Response

Here, Dr. Philips points to an instance in which a woman in the Old Testament "took her veil and covered herself." Dr. Philips does not state what he intends for this to prove, but it seems here that he believes that it intends to prove that God's law required women in the Old Testament to cover themselves. Of course, the text says no such thing. And if it is meant to state that an instance of a woman doing something in the Old Testament was evidence of God's law, then one could equally state that the fact that Rebekah was *not* covered before she "took her veil and covered herself" is evidence that God's law required that women not cover themselves. After all, Rebekah was not covered while she was speaking with her servant. Of course, Dr. Philips' premise is fundamentally flawed. If an instance of someone doing something in the Old Testament were evidence of God's law, then one could argue that God's law required eating of the forbidden fruit because there is an instance in the Old Testament where Eve ate of it.

c) Paul's Guidance on Veiling

(1) Overview

Dr. Philips writes (p. 86-87):

> Paul wrote in his first letter to the Corinthians [Chapter 11], "5 But any woman who prays or prophesies with her head unveiled dishonours her head-it is the same as if her head were shaven. 6 For if a woman will not veil herself, then she should cut off her hair, but if it is disgraceful for a woman to be shorn or shaven, let her wear a veil."

(2) Response 1: Paul's Instruction Reveals Local Culture

Paul's commentary in 1 Corinthians reflects not a biblical law requiring women to cover their hair, but local culture at the time, where a woman who does not veil herself, like a woman whose hair is shorn or whose head is shaved, is disgraced. He writes: "For if a woman is not covered, let her also be shorn. But if it is shameful for a woman to be shorn or shaved, let her be covered" (1Co 11:6). This disgrace of women who were unveiled or whose hair was shorn or heads was shaved was particular to the local culture at the time.

Dr. Philips denies that Paul's instruction reflected local culture at the time. He writes (p. 87):

> Some may argue that it was the general custom of those times to be completely veiled. However, that is not the case. In both Rome and Greece, whose cultures dominated the region, the popular dress was quite short and revealed the arms, legs and chest. Only religious women in Palestine, following Jewish tradition, covered themselves modestly.

Here, Dr. Philips conflates women's covering their hair with dressing modestly. The two are separate. Indeed, Paul instructs women to dress modestly elsewhere in the Bible. In 1 Timothy 2:9, he states his desire that "the women adorn themselves in modest apparel, with propriety and moderation, not with braided hair or gold or pearls or costly clothing." This is separate from the question of women's covering their hair. With respect to covering of hair, it is clear from the context that Paul instructs women to cover their hair because having an uncovered head during prayer or prophecy is the equivalent of having a shaved head (1Co 11:5), but it was at the time shameful for a woman to be shaved or shorn (1Co 11:6). Being shaved or shorn at the time was a sign of loose morals and sexual promiscuity and could have also indicated a refusal to submit to her husband. It may have also been a sign of prostitution. The commentary in the *NIV Study Bible* states (p. 1,748):

> For a woman, taking off her head covering in public and exposing her hair was a sign of loose morals and sexual promiscuity. Paul says she might as well have her hair cut or shaved off. The shaved head indicated that the woman either had been publicly disgraced because of some shameful act or was openly flaunting her independence and her refusal to be in submission to her husband. Paul's message to her was: Show your respect for and submission to your husband by covering your head during public worship.

(3) Response 2: If Paul's Instruction Did Not Reveal Local Culture, Then It Would Mean that Paul's Instruction Lined Up with God's Purported Will

It must be conceded that there are diverse interpretations of Paul's teaching in 1 Corinthians 11. Some suggest the fact that Paul references "nature" in 1 Corinthians 11:7-8 as evidence that women's covering their hair was a natural law principle rather than a requirement of local culture and tradition.

The commentary in the *NIV Study Bible* acknowledges multiple interpretations. It states (p. 1,748):

> Some do not see in these verses a temporary cultural significance to the covering/uncovering of the head. They insist that, since Paul referred to the order of creation (vv. 7-9), his directive is not to be restricted to his time. Thus women of all times should wear a head covering.

> Others find a lasting principle in the passage requiring wives, in all ways, to show respect for their husbands by submitting to their authority—not merely by a particular style of attire, but by godly lives. Man, who was created first, is to have authority over his wife (see 1Ti 2:11-14). The wife was made out of his body (Ge 2:21-24) to be his helper and companion (Ge 2:20). She is to honor her husband by submitting to him as her head (see v. 3).

> Still others see these verses, not as a mandate for all marriages, but as reflecting marriage relationships at that time in Corinth and therefore giving a reason why the women there should have covered their heads (v. 10). They point to vv. 11-12 as a contrast, emphasizing equality and mutual dependence between men and women who are "in the Lord" (v. 11; see Gal 3:28; 1Pe 3:7).

As discussed above, this study adopts the view that Paul's message on women's covering their heads reflects local custom. However, if that view is wrong and Paul's message in fact represented God's divine will rather than a reflection of local custom, this would undermine Dr. Philips' own argument. If God's will is that women cover their heads and Paul commanded this in 1 Corinthians, then it would confirm that Christianity reaffirms and complies with God's will. It would undermine Dr. Philips' argument that Christianity strays from God's will. All it would mean is that those women who do not cover their heads when they pray and prophesy were not complying with God's will. However, this is not an indication that the New Testament has gone astray; it is merely an indication that certain Christians are not complying with the New Testament.

The Qur'ān, in contrast, does not in any place clearly command that women must cover their heads or hair. Even the verse that Dr. Philips quotes, in 24:31 does not instruct women to cover their hair. It instructs them to "lower their gaze and protect their private parts and not to expose their adornment, except only what normally shows, and to draw their head-scarves over their bosoms." A woman can fully comply with this verse without ever drawing her headscarf over her hair.

d) Some Christian Churches Practice Veiling

Finally, Paul argues that certain Christian churches practicing veiling. He writes (p. 87):

> The famous early Christian theologian, St. Tertullian (d. 220 CE), in his famous treatise, 'On The Veiling of Virgins' wrote, "Young women, you wear your veils out on the streets, so you should wear them in the church; you wear them when you are among strangers, then wear them among your brothers."

It is unclear what Dr. Philips' point is here; if certain Christian churches practice veiling, then it would mean that Christianity has not departed from God's will. However, as stated above, veiling was never commanded or required by God. That certain Christian churches practice veiling is a reflection of local practice, custom and preference. Some churches sing hymns, while others do not; some use icons, while others do not; some serve communion every week, while others do not. The fact that there are variations among the practices of Christian churches is a testament to the diversity of Christian believers, , not that any one practice is demanded by God.

Dr. Philips also writes (p. 87):

> Among the Canon laws of the Catholic church until today, there is a law that requires women to cover their heads in church.

In support of his statement, he cites:

> Clara M. Henning, "Canon Law and the Battle of the Sexes," in *Religion and Sexism*, p. 272.

Although Dr. Philips fails to give the full citation, making it difficult for the reader to consult and confirm the reference, it appears that Dr. Philips is citing to Rosemary Radford Ruether's *Religion and Sexism: Images of Woman in the Jewish and Christian Traditions* (Simon & Schuster), which was published in 1974 and is out of print. However, an online copy[21] states on p. 272 the following with respect to the canon laws of the Catholic Church:

> It would be very hard to deny that the Church is intimately sexist. Sexist attitudes abound, reflected in laws, for example, that require women to cover their heads in church, discourage women from singing in Church, still prohibit women from approaching the altar during celebration, an do not admit girls or women as Mass servers.

It appears that Catholic canon law did at one point require women to cover their heads, and this was the case in 1974 when Rosemary Radford Ruether's *Religion and Sexism* was published. However, a new Code of Canon Law was promulgated in 1983 during the pontificate of John Paul II and abrogated the 1917 Code of Canon Law. The 193 Code of Canon Law permits, but does not require, women to wear chapel veils. This reflects the fact that covering one's head was intended not as an immutable divine law, but rather, as a practice that reflects local custom.

Dr. Philips also writes (p. 87):

> Christian denominations, such as the Amish and the Menonites for example, keep their women veiled to the present day.

Once again, the fact that certain denominations practice veiling does not mean that veiling is divinely mandated by God any more than having pews versus chairs in a sanctuary is divinely mandated. Some practices are reflective of custom or preference without being tied to divine law. If there *was* a divine law that mandated that women cover their heads, then at most, Dr. Philips' argument could be used to support the view that some Christian women follow it while others do not. It should be noted

---

[21] See
<https://books.google.com/books?id=9mhKAwAAQBAJ&pg=PA267&lpg=PA267&dq=clara+maria+henning+Canon+Law+and+the+Battle+of+the+Sexes&source=bl&ots=M4c6NL8ZVa&sig=ACfU3U3Uz9XxAcwPChUkDb_IR6JAqjQll g&hl=en&sa=X&ved=2ahUKEwi1tavmjN7pAhVYhXIEHb06CYgQ6AEwAXoECAkQAQ#v=onepage&q=clara%20maria%20henning%20Canon%20Law%20and%20the%20Battle%20of%20the%20Sexes&f=false>.

that the same is true of Muslim women—some cover their heads and others do not. At most, these facts support the conclusion that there are some women that obey God's law and others who do not, but ultimately, it cannot be used to argue the truth of a religion since, as Dr. Philips claims, both Islam and Christianity mandate that women cover their hair, though his interpretation of Paul's writings on headcovering is misguided.

8. Tithing

a) Overview

Dr. Philips writes that (p. 89):

> Jesus confirmed the institution of compulsory charity, known as "the tithe (tenth)", which was required from the annual harvest to be given back to God in celebration. In Deuteronomy 14:22: "You shall tithe all the yield of your seed, which comes forth from the field year by year."

Dr. Philips then quotes 6:141 of the Qur'ān to argue that the tithe continues in Islam (p. 89-90):

> "It is He who produces trellised and un-trellised gardens, date palms and crops of different shapes and tastes, and olives and pomegranates, similar yet different. Eat of their fruit when they bear, but pay the due at the time of harvest without being extravagant, for, surely He does not like those who are extravagant."

Finally, Dr. Philips equates the tithe with the *zakāt* charity (p. 90).

b) Response

Dr. Philips' arguments are flawed on several levels and demonstrate a misunderstanding of the nature of both the tithe and *zakāt*.

(1) Unlike the *Zakāt*, the Tithe Is Not Limited to the Yield of "Trellised and Un-trellised Gardens"

Unlike the "dues" in 6:141 of the Qur'ān, the tithe is not limited to a tenth of the harvest for "trellised and un-trellised gardens, date palms and crops of different shapes and tastes, and olives and pomegranates." The tithe applies to *everything* from the land, as well as to wine, oil and livestock. It applies to the following:

- A tithe (10%) of everything from the land (grain and fruit) (Lev 27:30), including a tithe of the produce of the year (Deu 14:28);
- The firstfruits of the ground, fruit, dough, offering, new wine and oil (Neh 10:35-39); and
- A tithe of the herd and flock (every tenth animal) (Lev 27:32-34).
- In some cases, the tithe consists of monetary currency if it is redeemed (Lev 27:31).
- The tithe that the Levites are to give to their priests consists of the best and holiest part of everything given to the Levites (Num 18:26-29), whether what is given is grain, fruit, livestock or currency.

(2) Unlike the *Zakāt*, the Tithe Applies to the "Increase," Not to Total Owned Property

The tithe applies to the "increase" that the fields produce (Deu 14:22; Deu 26:12). Unlike the *zakāt*, it is not a wealth tax. The *zakāt*, in contrast, applies to a Muslim's total wealth above a minimum amount (*niṣāb*).[22]

(3) Unlike the *Zakāt*, the Tithe is 10%, not 2.5%

Unlike the *zakāt*, which is customarily 2.5% (1/40) of a Muslim's total wealth,[23] the tithe is 10% of the increase (*i.e.*, income). In fact, the word "tithe" comes from the Old English *tēotha*, which in the ordinal sense means "tenth."

(4) Unlike the *Zakāt*, the Tithe Is Paid to the Levites and the Needy

The tithe is to be given to the Levites (Neh 10:35-39) or consumed by the Israelites (Deu 12:2-18, 14:22-27) and, in the third year, given to the Levite, the stranger, the orphan and the widow (Deu 14:28-29, 26:12-15). The *zakāt*, in contrast, should be paid to individuals or groups that fall into one or more of eight categories designated in the Qur'ān (9:60):

> Indeed, [prescribed] charitable offerings are only [to be given] to the poor and the indigent, and to those who work on [administering] it, and to those whose hearts are to be reconciled, and to [free] those in

---

[22] Yusuf al-Qaradawi, Monzer Kahf (transl.) *Fiqh az-Zakat*, Vol. 1 (London: Dar al Taqwa, 1999), pp. xxi–xxii.

[23] Muhammad Sarwar, *Al-Kafi*, Vol. 1 of 8 (Second ed.) (New York: The Islamic Seminary Inc., 2015), p. 345.

bondage, and to the debt-ridden, and for the cause of God, and to the wayfarer. [This is] an obligation from God. And God is all-knowing, all-wise. – Al-Tawbah, 9:60

These categories are as follows:
- the poor without means of livelihood;
- the needy who cannot meet their basic needs;
- *zakāt* collectors;
- those whose hearts are to be reconciled (*i.e.*, those sympathetic to or expected to convert to Islam, recent converts to Islam and potential allies in the cause of Islam);
- for freeing slaves;
- the debt-ridden;
- for the cause of Allāh and those fighting *jihād* by the pen, word or sword;
- to the stranded traveler.

c) Conclusion

Therefore, the charity commanded in verse 6:141 of the *Qur'ān* is distinct from the tithe commanded in Deuteronomy 14:22. Moreover, the Islamic institution of the *zakāt* is not a continuation of the biblical principle of tithing.

9. Fasting

a) Overview

Dr. Philips writes (p. 90):

> According to the Gospels, Jesus fasted for forty days. Matthew 4:2: "And he fasted forty days and forty nights, and afterward he was hungry." This was in accordance with the practice of the earlier prophets. Moses is also recorded in Exodus 34:28, to have fasted: "And he was there with the Lord forty days and forty nights; he neither ate bread nor drank water. And he wrote upon the tables the word of the covenant, the ten commandments."

Dr. Philips then quotes *sūra* 2:183 to support his contention that Muslims are also instructed to fast and writes that "believers are required to fast from dawn until dusk for the whole month of Ramadan (the ninth month of the lunar calendar)."

b) Response

To the extent that Islam teaches fasting generally, it is compatible with Christianity and Judaism. However, the specific fast commanded in the month of Ramadan every day from dawn to dusk has no precedent in Christianity or Judaism.

10. Prohibitions on Interest

a) Overview

Dr. Philips writes (p. 91):

> Prophet Jesus also opposed the giving or taking of interest because the texts of the Torah expressly forbade interest. It is recorded in Deuteronomy 23:19 that, "You shall not lend upon interest to your brother, interest on money, interest upon victuals, interest on anything that is lent for interest."

Dr. Philips then cites *sura* 2:278 of the *Qur'ān*, which also prohibits interest.

b) Response

Dr. Philips claims that Jesus opposed interest, but he gives no textual support for this other than his claim that "the Torah expressly forbade interest" (p. 91). However, there is no blanket prohibition on interest in the Torah. Rather, the prohibition is very specifically imposed on the charging of interest to fellow Israelites:

> Deu 23:19 "You shall not charge interest to your brother--interest on money or food or anything that is lent out at interest.

Dr. Philips cites Deuteronomy 23:19, but he conveniently omits from his treatise Deuteronomy 23:20, which expressly permits the Israelites to charge interest to foreigners:

> Deu 23:20 To a foreigner you may charge interest, but to your brother you shall not charge interest, that the Lord your God may bless you in all to which you set your hand in the land which you are entering to possess.

Therefore, if Jesus were, as Dr. Philips states, restating the Mosaic law, then he would have permitted interest among Gentiles and between

Israelites and Gentles. The blanket prohibition of interest in Islam, in contrast, would contravene the Mosaic law and Jesus's teachings.

11. Polygamy

Dr. Philips writes (p. 92-94):

> There is no record of Prophet Jesus opposing polygamy. If he did so, it would have meant that the condemned the practice of the prophets before him. There are a number of examples of polygamous marriages among the prophets recorded in the Torah.

He makes the following arguments in favor of polygamy, each of which we respond to and refute in turn.

a) Polygamous Patriarchs

(1) Overview

Dr. Philips cites the following examples:

- Abraham: "Then Sarai, Abram's wife, took Hagar her maid, the Egyptian, and gave her to her husband Abram to be his wife, after Abram had dwelt ten years in the land of Canaan" (Gen 16:3; miscited by Dr. Philips as Gen 16:13).
- David: "So David dwelt with Achish at Gath, he and his men, each man with his household, and David with his two wives, Ahinoam the Jezreelitess, and Abigail the Carmelitess, Nabal's widow" (1Sa 27:3). In addition, David married Michael, daughter of Saul, Bathsheba, the widow of Uriah the Hittite, Maacah, Haggith, Abital, and Eglah.
- Solomon: "And he had seven hundred wives, princesses, and three hundred concubines; and his wives turned away his heart" (1Ki 11:3).
- Rehoboam, son of Solomon: "Now Rehoboam loved Maachah the granddaughter of Absalom more than all his wives and his concubines; for he took eighteen wives and sixty concubines, and begot twenty-eight sons and sixty daughters" (2Ch 11:21).

In addition, Dr. Philips states that Jacob had four wives, in keeping with the Talmud (p. 93).

(2) Response

The following sections discuss each instance of polygamy on the part of the Patriarchs that Dr. Philips cites. As will be seen, these polygamous marriages are disastrous and indicative of sin or disobedience on some level. They either reflect a lack of faith in God, outright sin or pain or emotional toil and suffering.

(a) Abraham

(i) Overview

Abraham was married to Sarah and Hagar simultaneously in a bigamous marriage. After Sarah died, he then married Keturah. God promised Abraham that he would have descendants as numerous as the stars:

> Gen 15:2 But Abram said, "Lord GOD, what will You give me, seeing I go childless, and the heir of my house is Eliezer of Damascus?"

> Gen 15:3 Then Abram said, "Look, You have given me no offspring; indeed one born in my house is my heir!"

> Gen 15:4 And behold, the word of the Lord came to him, saying, "This one shall not be your heir, but one who will come from your own body shall be your heir."

> Gen 15:5 Then He brought him outside and said, "Look now toward heaven, and count the stars if you are able to number them." And He said to him, "So shall your descendants be."

> Gen 15:6 And he believed in the Lord, and He accounted it to him for righteousness.

Sarah gave Abraham her maidservant Hagar to be his wife. Abraham succumbed:

> Gen 16:1 Now Sarai, Abram's wife, had borne him no children. And she had an Egyptian maidservant whose name was Hagar.

> Gen 16:2 So Sarai said to Abram, "See now, the Lord has restrained me from bearing children. Please, go in to my maid; perhaps I shall obtain children by her." And Abram heeded the voice of Sarai.

> Gen 16:3 Then Sarai, Abram's wife, took Hagar her maid, the Egyptian, and gave her to her husband Abram to be his wife, after Abram had dwelt ten years in the land of Canaan.

(ii) Lack of Faith

There is an implication that Sarah's giving of Hagar to Abraham to be his wife is indicative of a lack of faith in God's promise that Abraham would bear descendants as numerous as the "stars" (Gen 15:5). Perhaps Sarah got tired of waiting and decided it was time for her to take action into her own hands, that if God had not yet delivered on His promise that it was time for her ingenuity to bring about God's plan in her timing. Sarah likely knew that marriage was a covenant, and that God had made the promise to Abraham at the time he was married to Sarah, and therefore that the promise should have been read as meaning that Abraham would have children through his covenant wife, not through plural marriage. Yet Sarah, rushing God's plan, gave Abraham Hagar to bear children rather than await God's plan to be fulfilled through her.

(iii) Emotional Turmoil

The fact that Abraham's taking of Hagar as his wife was an instance of sinfulness is made evidence by the fruit that immediately followed from the marriage and bearing of Ishmael. The marriage led to emotional turmoil and envy on the part of Sarah and strife between Hagar and Sarah, who dealt harshly with Hagar:

> Gen 16:4 So he went in to Hagar, and she conceived. And when she saw that she had conceived, her mistress became despised in her eyes.

> Gen 16:5 Then Sarai said to Abram, "My wrong be upon you! I gave my maid into your embrace; and when she saw that she had conceived, I became despised in her eyes. The Lord judge between you and me."

> Gen 16:6 So Abram said to Sarai, "Indeed your maid is in your hand; do to her as you please." And when Sarai dealt harshly with her, she fled from her presence.

Such strife and emotional turmoil is typical in plural marriages.

(b) Jacob

(i) Jacob Had Two, Not Four Wives

Dr. Philips' first error is to claim that Jacob had four wives. In fact, he had only two wives—Leah and Rachel. The other two—Bilpah and Zilpah—were concubines rather than wives joined to him in marriage.

Rachel gave Jacob her maid Bilhah to bear children (Gen 30:3-4). While Bilpah can be characterized as a "wife," she was, more accurately, a concubine who never married Jacob. The same is true of Zilpah, Leah's made that Leah gave to Jacob as his wife (Gen 30:9) to bear him children (Gen 30:10).

Therefore, Jacob had two wives and two concubines.

(ii) The Number of Wives Permitted by the Talmud

Second, Dr. Philips fails to support his claim that "the Talmud advises a maximum of four wives" (p. 93). He provides the reference "*Women in Judaism,* p. 148," but does not provide the full bibliographical data of the book, which does not appear to exist in online searches or in book catalogues. Therefore, the reader is rendered unable to verify the quotation or review its full context.

(iii)Jacob's Marriage to Leah Was a Result of Sinful Deceit and Greed on the Part of Laban

Jacob did not marry Leah and Rachel because he was following a prototype for marriage designed by God. He married Leah and Rachel because he was tricked by his father-in-law. Jacob agreed to work for his uncle Laban for seven years in exchange for marriage to Laban's younger daughter Rachel (Gen 29:16-20). After seven years, Jacob demanded his wife (Gen 29:21), but Laban gave Jacob his older daughter Leah instead (Gen 29:23-34). The next morning, Jacob learned that he laid with Leah, not Rachel (Gen 29:25). Jacob protested and Laban told him to consummate Leah's bridal week and he would then give him Rachel in marriage in exchange for another seven years of work. Jacob agreed (Gen 29:26-30). Therefore, Jacob's plural marriage was due to Laban's deceit and greed, hardly qualities that God encourages.

(iv)Jacob's Polygamy Led to Pain and Emotional Turmoil

In the case of Jacob, polygamy led to pain, pain, emotional toil and suffering. Jacob was tricked by his uncle Laban into marrying Leah, a woman he did not love. After agreeing to work for his uncle Laban for seven years in exchange for marriage to Laban's Rachel (Gen 29:16-20), Jacob demanded his wife following his seven years of labor (Gen 29:21), but Laban gave Jacob his older daughter Leah instead (Gen 29:23-34). Laban told Jacob that he would give him Rachel in marriage in exchange for another seven years of work, and Jacob agreed (Gen 29:26-30).

The bigamy led to heartbreak and envy. Leah was not loved, so God opened her womb to bear a son named Reuben (Gen 29:31-32) and later Simeon (Gen 29:33), Levi (Gen 29:34) and Judah (Gen 29:35). Rachel bore no children and thus envied Leah (Gen 30:1). The bigamy was the result of Laban's deceit, which was the direct cause of the envy and heartbreak that characterized the bigamous marriage.

(c) David

(i) Overview of David's Polygamy

The Bible names seven women as David's spouses, though it is possible that he had more. 1 Chronicles 3 lists David's descendants for 30 generations. This source names seven wives:

- Ahinoam of Jezreel
- Abigail the Carmel
- Maachah the daughter of King Talmai of Geshur
- Haggith
- Abital
- Eglah
- Bath-shua (Bathsheba) the daughter of Ammiel

David was married to Ahinoam, Abigail, Maacha, Haggith, Abital, and Eglah during the 7-1/2 years he reigned in Hebron as king of Judah. David married Bathsheba after he moved his capital to Jerusalem. Each of his first six wives bore David a son and Bathsheba bore him four sons.

The 1 Chronicles 3 account does not list Michal, daughter of King Saul, as one of David's wives. However, her marriage to David is recorded in 1 Samuel 18:27 ("Then Saul gave him Michal his daughter as a wife"). Her omission from the genealogy in 1 Chronicles 3 may be linked to 2 Samuel 6:23, which says, "to her dying day Michal, daughter of Saul, had no children."

(ii) David's Polygamy Was Marked by Sin

At least one of David's marriages—his marriage to Bathsheba—was marked by the sins of lust, adultery and murder. David went up to the roof of his house one evening and from the roof, he saw Bathsheba, the wife of Uriah the Hittite, bathing (2Sa 11:2-3) and lusted after her. Then

David sent messengers to bring her and he lay with her (2Sa 11:4). She conceived (2Sa 11:5) and David sent for her husband Uriah (2Sa 11:6), expecting Uriah to lie with Bathsheba, but Uriah did not (2Sa 11:9) because Israel was in battle (2Sa 11:11). King David wrote a letter commanding Joab to put David at the forefront of the battle so that he would be struck down and die (2Sa 11:15-15), which Joab did, and Uriah died (2Sa 11:16-17). David thus had Uriah killed to cover up his sins of lust and adultery. After Bathsheba mourned for the death of Uriah (2Sa 11:26), she became David's wife and bore him a son (2Sa 11:27).

Nathan came to David and told him of a rich man with who had many flocks and herds and a poor man who had only one little ewe lamb. When a visitor came to the rich man, the rich man refused to take from his own flock to serve him, so he took the poor man's lamb and prepared it for his visitor (2Sa 12:1-4).

When David's anger was aroused (2Sa 12:5), Nathan told him that he (David) was the rich man (2Sa 12:7) and that as a result of David's sin, the sword will never depart from David's house and God will raise up adversity against David and will take his wives and give them to his neighbor, who will do in the open before all Israel what David did in secret (2Sa 12:10-12).

David recognized that he "sinned against the Lord" (2Sa 12:13). Nathan declared that David's child by Bathsheba child would die (2Sa 12:14). The Lord struck David's child with an illness (2Sa 12:15). David fasted and prayed (2Sa 12:16), but the child died after seven days of illness (2Sa 12:18).

(d) Solomon

In the case of Solomon, polygamy led to outright sin and idolatry. King Solomon loved many foreign women, as well as the daughter of Pharaoh and women of the Moabites, Ammonites, Edomites, Sidonians and Hittites (1Ki 11:1). He loved women of whom the Lord said, "You shall not intermarry with them, nor they with you; surely they will turn away your hearts after their gods" (1Ki 11:2). He had seven hundred wives, princesses, and three hundred concubines; and his wives turned his heart after other gods; and his heart was not loyal to the Lord (1Ki 11:3-4).

Solomon built a high place for Chemosh, the god of Moab, and for Molech, the god of Ammon (1Ki 11:7), so God became angry with Solomon (1Ki 11:9) and said to him, "Because you have done this, and have not kept My covenant and My statutes, which I have commanded you, I will surely tear the kingdom away from you and give it to your servant. Nevertheless I will not do it in your days, for the sake of your father David; I will tear it out of the hand of your son. However I will not tear away the whole kingdom; I will give one tribe to your son for the sake of my servant David, and for the sake of Jerusalem which I have chosen" (1Ki 11:11-13).

(e) Noah as a Foil to the Polygamists

Noah serves as a foil whose monogamous marriage stands in contrast to the polygamous failed marriages of other patriarchs and of his own father, Lamech. The first instance of polygamy in the Bible appears after the entry of sin into the world with the fall of Adam and Eve through Lamech, who married two wives—Adah and Zillah (Gen 4:19).

One can compare the qualities of Lamech, a murderer (Gen 4:23) and polygamist (Gen 4:19), with those of Lamech's son, Noah, a righteous man who had only one wife (Gen 7:7). Noah found grace in the eyes of God (Gen 6:8) and was a righteous man who was perfect in his generation and walked with God (Gen 6:9). The fact that the Bible highlights a man in a monogamous marriage as a "righteous" and "perfect" man underscores monogamy as the model that God intended for marriage.

b) Old Testament Laws Governing Polygamy

(1) Overview

Dr. Philips then points out that "the Torah even specified laws regarding the division of inheritance in polygamous circumstances" (p. 92) (Deu 21:15-16):

> Deu 21:15 "If a man has two wives, one loved and the other unloved, and they have borne him children, both the loved and the unloved, and if the firstborn son is of her who is unloved,

> Deu 21:16 then it shall be, on the day he bequeaths his possessions to his sons, that he must not bestow firstborn status on the son of the loved wife in preference to the son of the unloved, the true firstborn.

"The only restriction on polygamy was the ban on taking a wife's sister as a rival wife" (p. 93) (Lev 18:18):

Lev 18:18 Nor shall you take a woman as a rival to her sister, to uncover her nakedness while the other is alive.

(2) Response

(a) Polygamy is Regulated but Not Encouraged or Blessed in the Old Testament

The Old Testament laws on polygamy should not be viewed as permitting or giving God's blessing to polygamy. Rather, they should be viewed as restrictions on a sinful institution to make it less sinful.

(b) Polygamy Is Like the Monarchy, Which Was Regulated but Not Blessed by God

Polygamy is similar to the institution of the monarchy, which God only reluctantly allowed for Israel and only after Israel insisted on having a king like the other nations.

> 1Sa 8:5 and said to him, "Look, you are old, and your sons do not walk in your ways. Now make us a king to judge us like all the nations."
>
> 1Sa 8:6 But the thing displeased Samuel when they said, "Give us a king to judge us." So Samuel prayed to the Lord.
>
> 1Sa 8:7 And the Lord said to Samuel, "Heed the voice of the people in all that they say to you; for they have not rejected you, but they have rejected Me, that I should not reign over them.
>
> 1Sa 8:8 According to all the works which they have done since the day that I brought them up out of Egypt, even to this day—with which they have forsaken Me and served other gods—so they are doing to you also.
>
> 1Sa 8:9 Now therefore, heed their voice. However, you shall solemnly forewarn them, and show them the behavior of the king who will reign over them."
>
> 1Sa 8:10 So Samuel told all the words of the Lord to the people who asked him for a king.
>
> 1Sa 8:11 And he said, "This will be the behavior of the king who will reign over you: He will take your sons and appoint them for his

own chariots and to be his horsemen, and some will run before his chariots.

1Sa 8:12 He will appoint captains over his thousands and captains over his fifties, will set some to plow his ground and reap his harvest, and some to make his weapons of war and equipment for his chariots.

1Sa 8:13 He will take your daughters to be perfumers, cooks, and bakers.

1Sa 8:14 And he will take the best of your fields, your vineyards, and your olive groves, and give them to his servants.

1Sa 8:15 He will take a tenth of your grain and your vintage, and give it to his officers and servants.

1Sa 8:16 And he will take your male servants, your female servants, your finest young men, and your donkeys, and put them to his work.

1Sa 8:17 He will take a tenth of your sheep. And you will be his servants.

1Sa 8:18 And you will cry out in that day because of your king whom you have chosen for yourselves, and the Lord will not hear you in that day."

1Sa 8:19 Nevertheless the people refused to obey the voice of Samuel; and they said, "No, but we will have a king over us,

1Sa 8:20 that we also may be like all the nations, and that our king may judge us and go out before us and fight our battles."

1Sa 8:21 And Samuel heard all the words of the people, and he repeated them in the hearing of the Lord.

1Sa 8:22 So the Lord said to Samuel, "Heed their voice, and make them a king." And Samuel said to the men of Israel, "Every man go to his city."

God instituted limitations as to the qualifications of the king not because the monarchy was His will from the start, but because He wanted to place limitations on a sinful institution:

Deu 17:14 "When you come to the land which the Lord your God is giving you, and possess it and dwell in it, and say, 'I will set a king over me like all the nations that are around me,'

Deu 17:15 you shall surely set a king over you whom the Lord your God chooses; one from among your brethren you shall set as king over you; you may not set a foreigner over you, who is not your brother.

Deu 17:16 But he shall not multiply horses for himself, nor cause the people to return to Egypt to multiply horses, for the Lord has said to you, 'You shall not return that way again.'

Deu 17:17 Neither shall he multiply wives for himself, lest his heart turn away; nor shall he greatly multiply silver and gold for himself.

Deu 17:18 "Also it shall be, when he sits on the throne of his kingdom, that he shall write for himself a copy of this law in a book, from the one before the priests, the Levites.

Deu 17:19 And it shall be with him, and he shall read it all the days of his life, that he may learn to fear the Lord his God and be careful to observe all the words of this law and these statutes,

Deu 17:20 that his heart may not be lifted above his brethren, that he may not turn aside from the commandment to the right hand or to the left, and that he may prolong his days in his kingdom, he and his children in the midst of Israel.

(c) Polygamy Is Like Divorce, Which Was Regulated but Not Blessed By God

In the Old Testament, an Israelite man may divorce a foreign captive woman whom he has married if she does not please him. She is then free to go where she wishes, with the implication that she may remarry (Deu 21:10-14). The law prohibits the sale and brutal treatment of such women. The law also permits an Israelite man to divorce a woman of his own nationality and status:

Deu 24:1 "When a man takes a wife and marries her, and it happens that she finds no favor in his eyes because he has found some uncleanness in her, and he writes her a certificate of divorce, puts it in her hand, and sends her out of his house,

Deu 24:2 when she has departed from his house, and goes and becomes another man's wife,

Deu 24:3 if the latter husband detests her and writes her a certificate of divorce, puts it in her hand, and sends her out of his house, or if the latter husband dies who took her as his wife,

Deu 24:4 then her former husband who divorced her must not take her back to be his wife after she has been defiled; for that is an abomination before the Lord, and you shall not bring sin on the land which the Lord your God is giving you as an inheritance.

Jesus made clear that although the Mosaic law imposed regulations on divorce, divorce was never God's will. The purpose of the regulations was to protect the rights of divorced women. When he was challenged by the Pharisees on this question, Jesus likened divorce to adultery :

Mat 19:3 The Pharisees also came to Him, testing Him, and saying to Him, "Is it lawful for a man to divorce his wife for just any reason?"

...

Mat 19:7 They said to Him, "Why then did Moses command to give a certificate of divorce, and to put her away?"

Mat 19:8 He said to them, "Moses, because of the hardness of your hearts, permitted you to divorce your wives, but from the beginning it was not so.

Mat 19:9 And I say to you, whoever divorces his wife, except for sexual immorality, and marries another, commits adultery; and whoever marries her who is divorced commits adultery."

c) What the New Testament States

(1) Overview

Dr. Philips quotes Father Eugene Hillman as stating that "[n]owhere in the New Testament is there any explicit commandment that marriage should be monogamous or any explicit commandment forbidding polygamy" (p. 93).

(2) Response

Dr. Philips' arguments are flawed on multiple levels. As with his reliance on the book *Women in Judaism*, Dr. Philips fails to provide the full bibliographical data of the book *Polygamy Reconsidered*, which does not appear to exist in online searches or in book catalogues. Therefore, the reader is unable to verify the quotation or review its full context.

However, assuming that Dr. Philips faithfully quotes from the book, the quotation is not appurtenant. To justify marriage on the basis that "nowhere in the New Testament is there an explicit prohibition on polygamy" is like stating that marriage between a man and an orangutan is permitted because "nowhere in the New Testament is there an explicit prohibition on marriage between a man and an orangutan."

More importantly, the quotation upon which Dr. Philips relies makes a false claim. The New Testament very clearly discourages polygamy. The Epistles alone contain three explicit statements that church leaders, who are to be examples for the congregation, should be the "husband of one wife":

- 1Ti 3:2 A bishop then must be blameless, the *husband of one wife*, temperate, sober-minded, of good behavior, hospitable, able to teach;
- 1Ti 3:12 Let deacons be the *husbands of one wife*, ruling their children and their own houses well;
- Tit 1:5 For this reason I left you in Crete, that you should set in order the things that are lacking, and appoint elders in every city as I commanded you--Tit 1:6 if a man is blameless, the *husband of one wife*, having faithful children not accused of dissipation or insubordination.

d) Dr. Philips Contradicts Himself Regarding Polygamy Practices by Old Testament Prophets and Islam's Restriction of Up to Four Wives

(1) Overview

Dr. Philips writes that if Jesus opposed polygamy, "it would have meant that the [sic] condemned the practice of the prophets before him" (p. 92). Here, Dr. Philips implies that by His silence, Jesus condoned or even ratified the polygamy of earlier prophets, including Abraham, Jacob, David, Solomon and Rehoboam, all of whom Dr. Philips explicitly mentions as polygamous. With respect to Solomon, Dr. Philips quotes 1 Kings 11:3, which states that he had seven hundred wives, princesses and three hundred concubines." Therefore, by not opposing polygamy, Jesus implicitly condoned Solomon's 700 wives.

However, Dr. Philips then writes (p. 93-94):

Islaam limited polygamy to a maximum of four wives at one time and stipulated the maintenance of justice as a basic condition for polygamy. In Chapter an-Nisaa (4):3, God states:

"Marry of the women that please you two, three or four. But if you fear that you will not be able to deal justly, then [marry only] one ..."

(2) Response

If by His silence, Jesus condoned and ratified polygamy, and Solomon, as a prophet who, according to Islam, was sinless,[24] married 700 wives, then on what authority could Muhammad, who supposedly ratified and reinstated the message of earlier prophets, change the practice of polygamy by limiting it to only four wives? Was Solomon incompliant with Allāh's restriction on plural marriage to a limit of four wives? Or did Allāh initially allow up to 700 wives and concubines and then later change his mind and limit it to four? If the restriction on four wives was always in place, then Solomon sinfully transgressed Allāh's law. If that is the case, then how could Solomon be a prophet when, according to Islam, prophets could not sin?

Some Muslims might respond that Allāh changed his law. This, in turn, leads to other problematic issues, including how an unchanging god can change his law in evident self-contradictions. If that is possible, then what other contradictions are possible?

e) *Monogamous Marriage Was Instituted in the Creation of Adam and Eve*

Monogamous marriage was instituted in the creation of Adam and Eve. God crated them as one husband and one wife. He created Adam and Eve, not Adam and Eve and Eva and Fatima and Khadija. God

---

[24] *See* "Do Prophets sin? Do they need forgiveness?" *Islam Question & Answer* <https://islamqa.info/en/answers/1684/do-prophets-sin-do-they-need-forgiveness> ("The ummah (Muslim nation) is agreed that the Messengers are infallible in carrying out their mission they do not forget anything that Allaah has revealed to them except with regard to matters that have been abrogated"); "Did the Prophet (peace and blessings of Allaah be upon him) commit sin?" *Islam Question & Answer* <https://islamqa.info/en/answers/7208/did-the-prophet-peace-and-blessings-of-allaah-be-upon-him-commit-sin> ("sin (khatee'ah, pl. khataayaa) is impossible in the case of the Messengers").

specifically instituted marriage between a man and his "wife," not "wives" (Gen 2:24):

> Gen 2:23 And Adam said: "This is now bone of my bones And flesh of my flesh; She shall be called Woman, Because she was taken out of Man."

> Gen 2:24 Therefore a man shall leave his father and mother and be joined to his wife, and they shall become one flesh.

> Gen 2:25 And they were both naked, the man and his wife, and were not ashamed.

Chapter 5. Denying Jesus' Divinity

A. Verses that Appear to Deny Jesus' Divinity

1. Jesus Allegedly Denied Being "Good"

a) *Argument*

On two occasions in the book, Dr. Philips cites Jesus when He responds to the rich young man's questions about inheriting eternal life. The first is on pages 37-38:

> [I]n Matthew 19:17, Jesus responded to one who addressed him as "O good master", saying: "Why callest thou me good? There is none good but one. that is God." If he rejected being called "good", and stated that only God is truly good, he clearly implies that he is not God.

The second is on page 67:

> In Matthew 19: 16-17, when the man called Prophet Jesus 'good', saying, "Good teacher, what good thing shall I do that I may have eternal life?" Prophet Jesus replied, "Why do you call me good? No one is good but One, that is, God." He denied the attribution of 'infinite goodness' or 'perfect goodness' to himself, and affirmed that this attribute belongs to Allaah alone.

b) *Response 1*

The error with this argument is that it presumes that Jesus rejected being called "good." However, nowhere in the Bible does Jesus reject being good. He merely asks the young man a question, "Why do you call Me good?" (Mat 19:17). He then states that only God is good. If only God is good, then Jesus cannot be good *unless he is God.* In his conversation with the young man, Jesus neither denies being good nor does he deny being God. Instead, He affirms throughout the New

Testament that He is God and the Son of God.[25] Therefore, Matthew 19:17, taken in context, should be interpreted to be yet another affirmation by Jesus that He is God. In asking the young man why he called Jesus "good," and proclaiming that only God was good, Jesus was challenging the young man to consider the implications of what He was saying and to recognize that Jesus was, in fact, God.

c) Response 2

In addition to the above response, a second response can be made on the basis of the original manuscripts on which Matthew 19:16-17 is based. The text that is quoted by Dr. Philips has Jesus responding by saying, "Why callest thou me good?" It is based on the KJV, which states, in its full context:

> Mat 19:16 And, behold, one came and said unto him, Good Master, what good thing shall I do, that I may have eternal life?
>
> Mat 19:17 And he said unto him, Why callest thou me good? there is none good but one, that is, God: but if thou wilt enter into life, keep the commandments.

The KJV text is based on the *Textus Receptus*, which is a late text that was compiled in the 16th century. However, in the 19th and 20th centuries, much older and more reliable manuscripts have come to light. More modern translations, such as the NIV, NASB, and the RSV/NRSV, draw on the witness of these manuscripts in their translations. The NIV translates Matthew 19:16-17 as follows:

> Mat 19:16 Just then a man came up to Jesus and asked, "Teacher, what good thing must I do to get eternal life?"
>
> Mat 19:17 "Why do you ask me about what is good?" Jesus replied. "There is only One who is good. If you want to enter life, keep the commandments."

In this translation, Jesus' emphasis is not on His own goodness, but rather, on the concept of goodness proper. He challenges the rich young man to consider what he is asking, *i.e.*, why are you asking me about

---

[25] See, for example, Matthew 26:63-64, where Jesus affirmed before the High Priest that He is the Son of God, and Matthew 16:16-17, where Peter affirmed that Jesus is the Son of God and Jesus praised Peter for his faith.

what is good? Do you not realize that you cannot be good, because only God is good? Jesus instructs the rich young man, stating:

> Mat 19:18 "'You shall not murder, you shall not commit adultery, you shall not steal, you shall not give false testimony,

> Mat 19:19 honor your father and mother,' and 'love your neighbor as yourself.'"

However, Jesus did not end there. It was not enough to follow the commandments of the Old Testament. He went on to instruct the rich young man as to what he needed to do in order to become perfect:

> Mat 19:21 "If you want to be perfect, go, sell your possessions and give to the poor, and you will have treasure in heaven. Then come, follow me."

Jesus calls us to go beyond following the commandments; He calls us to "be perfect" and "follow me." We are called to become His followers and disciples, and only then do we become "good." So in questioning the rich young man, Jesus is not stating that He is not good. Rather, He is challenging the young man to recognize that only God (and Jesus, who is God in essence) is good, and that we can only become good by following Jesus.

2. If Jesus Were God, He Would Be Omniscient; Yet He Did Not Know When Heaven and Earth Would Pass Away

a) Argument

Dr. Philips writes that if Jesus were God, He would be omniscient (p. 39). However, in Mark 13:31-32, Jesus said that He did not know the hour when heaven and earth will pass away:

> Mark 13:31 Heaven and earth will pass away, but My words will by no means pass away.

> Mark 13:32 "But of that day and hour no one knows, not even the angels in heaven, nor the Son, but only the Father.

In Matthew, Jesus's words are similar:

> Mat 24:35 Heaven and earth will pass away, but My words will by no means pass away.

> Mat 24:36 "But of that day and hour no one knows, not even the angels of heaven, but My Father only.

On this basis, we must conclude that Jesus and the Father are not one. The natural conclusion to this is that the Father, who is God, is omniscient, and Jesus, who is a man, is not omniscient.

b) *Response 1: While Jesus Walked on the Earth, He Was Not Fully God*

(1) Overview

One possible explanation for Mark 13:32 and Matthew 24:36 is that Jesus, who is one with God and the Father, and by His divine nature omnipotent, omniscient, and omnipresent, gave up his divine powers, and humbled Himself to become man, undergo human temptation and suffering, and suffer as a man for the salvation of the world. As Paul wrote in his Letter to the Philippians:

> Php 2:5 Let this mind be in you which was also in Christ Jesus,
>
> Php 2:6 who, being in the form of God, did not consider it robbery to be equal with God,
>
> Php 2:7 but made Himself of no reputation, taking the form of a bondservant, and coming in the likeness of men.
>
> Php 2:8 And being found in appearance as a man, He humbled Himself and became obedient to the point of death, even the death of the cross.

(2) Problem with Proposed Explanation

This view assumes that while Jesus walked on the earth as man incarnate, He was not fully God. However, such a view violates the principle of the immutability of God, as memorialized in Malachi 3:6 ("For I am the Lord, I do not change") and Hebrews 13:8 ("Jesus Christ is the same yesterday, today, and forever").

c) *Response 2: Jesus Continued to Be Omniscient as God, But While He Was a Man, an Attribute Was Added to Him*

(1) Overview

Dr. Jack Cottrell attempts to circumvent the immutability issue by arguing that when "the Word became flesh" (John 1:14),[26]

> there was no change in the essence—the attributes—of the Logos. He did not surrender or give up anything; rather, He ADDED something. The incarnation was accomplished not by subtraction from the divine nature but by the adding or joining of human nature to the divine. This would have made profound differences in God's experiences and consciousness and actions, but not in his essence.

(2) Problem with Proposed Explanation

Dr. Cottrell is essentially playing a game of semantics. He attempts to get around the change in Jesus's immutability by characterizing Jesus's loss of omniscience as an added attribute rather than as a changed attribute. He acknowledges that the following formulation would be a change in Jesus's character that unacceptably contravenes his immutability as God:

- Jesus is omniscient God.
- Then He becomes man not possessing omniscience during the time He walked on the earth.

Dr. Cottrell circumvents this problem by arguing the following:

- Jesus is omniscient God.
- He then gains the attribute of finite manhood during the time He walked on the earth.
- The lack of omniscience of His human nature cancels out his divine omniscience.

Essentially, Dr. Cottrell is arguing for a chance in Jesus's omniscience, but rather than characterize it as a change, he characterizes it as an added attribute. However, the net effect is the same: Jesus's knowledge transforms goes from unlimited omniscience to finite knowledge. Regardless of whether it is characterized as a loss of omniscience or the adding of the attribute of limited human knowledge, it constitutes a change in Jesus's character that contradicts the immutability of God.

---

[26] "Was Jesus Omniscient?" (18 June 2014), available at <http://jackcottrell.com/uncategorized/was-jesus-omniscient>.

d) Response 3: Jesus Gave Up the Use of His Omniscience

(1) Overview

Next, Dr. Cottrell argues that Jesus in fact remained omniscient, but in His humanity, He[27]:

> voluntarily gave up the USE of some of His divine attributes. This was not a diminishing of His divine nature but a veiling of it, which consisted of a temporary suspension of the exercise of His prerogatives as God. As a nativity hymn says, "Veiled in flesh the Godhead see! Hail, incarnate deity!" This is why much of His messianic work was accomplished via the strengthening presence of the Holy Spirit.

The idea that Jesus remained omniscient but gave up the use of his omniscience is not beyond the realm of reason. It can be argued, for example, that Jesus remained omnipotent during his earthly ministry, but He declined to rescue Himself from the cross. Many blasphemed Him and said "You who destroy the temple and build it in three days, save Yourself! If You are the Son of God, come down from the cross" (Mat 27:39-40), yet Jesus, in order to fulfill God's will, refused to do so.

(2) Problem with Proposed Explanation

There is a problem with the proposed explanation because there is a fundamental difference between power and knowledge. Suspending the use of power in no way undermines the existence of that power. However, suspending knowledge cannot be compatible with possessing knowledge. One either knows something or he does not. If he does not know it, he cannot be omniscient. It cannot be said that Jesus was all-knowing and yet he suspended his omniscience when he became a man. If he suspended his omniscience, then He was not all-knowing. Clearly, this is the case because Jesus did not know the hour that heaven and earth would pass away. It is not possible to have knowledge and then suspend it. Unlike power, which can be had and not used, one either has or does not have knowledge, regardless of whether it is used.

---

[27] "Was Jesus Omniscient?" (18 June 2014), available at <http://jackcottrell.com/uncategorized/was-jesus-omniscient>.

e) Response 4: Jesus Remained Omniscient, but Suspended Use of His Omniscience

Next, Dr. Cottrell argues that in fact, Jesus remained omniscient, even during his earthly ministry, but did not "will" Himself to know the hour that heaven and earth would pass away. Dr. Cottrell first provides examples to demonstrate Jesus's omniscience[28]:

- Jesus knew the secret contents of men's hearts, which 1 John 3:20 suggests is a prerogative of deity: "For God is greater than our heart and knows all things."
- On one occasion the Jewish leaders were thinking accusing thoughts of Jesus, and Mark 2:8 says that "immediately Jesus [was] aware in His spirit that they were reasoning that way within themselves." He was "knowing their thoughts" (Matt. 9:4; see Matt. 12:25).
- On another occasion of potential conflict with the scribes and Pharisees, "He knew what they were thinking" (Luke 6:8; see also 9:47).
- John 2:24 says, "He knew all men."
- On several occasions, Jesus exhibited foreknowledge, which as per Isaiah 46:9-10 ("I am God, and there is none like Me, Declaring the end from the beginning, And from ancient times things that are not yet done"), is an attribute of God.
  - o He knew that Judas would betray Him: "For Jesus knew from the beginning who they were who did not believe, and who it was that would betray Him" (John 6:64).
  - o On the night before His death, He said to Peter, "Before a rooster crows twice, you will deny Me three times" (Mark 14:72).
- Jesus' disciples noted His divine knowledge: "Now we know that You know all things, and have no need for anyone to question You; by this we believe that You came from God" (John 16:30).
- Peter acknowledged, "Lord, You know all things" (John 21:17).

Despite Jesus's omniscience, He willed not to use it with respect to the hour of His return[29]:

---

[28] "Was Jesus Omniscient?" (18 June 2014), available at <http://jackcottrell.com/uncategorized/was-jesus-omniscient>.
[29] "Was Jesus Omniscient?" (18 June 2014), available at <http://jackcottrell.com/uncategorized/was-jesus-omniscient>.

As a result of the incarnation, the divine nature (the Logos) and the human nature of Jesus shared one stream of consciousness and one moment of awareness at any given time. As we would say about ourselves, we can be thinking of only one thing at a time. I believe this applied to Jesus. His human nature dictated that He be conscious of only one thing at a time. But here is the difference between Him and us: as the omniscient divine Logos, He could will Himself to know (be conscious of) any knowledge-content that he chose to know. He could choose to know the heart of any individual, but He was not consciously thinking about it all the time. Likewise, He could have chosen to know the time of the second coming, but it was the decision of divine wisdom that as the man Jesus Christ He did NOT choose to bring this datum to his consciousness, and for our sake He told us that this was the case (in Matt. 24:36)! The benefit of this is that we know that it is vain to search the sayings of Jesus as recorded in the Gospels for some secret, hidden hint as to the time of His return.

This proposed explanation is not without reason, if we accept that Jesus was both omniscient and omnipotent. Being omnipotent, He could control all things, including what He knew and did not know. Therefore, He could possess all knowledge, yet will Himself not to have a particular datum in his consciousness. He could thus hold the ability to know the hour that heaven and earth will pass away, just has He had the ability to lower Himself from the cross, yet He willed Himself not to know it because it was the Father's prerogative, just as it was the Father's will to give His only Son to die on the cross (John 3:16), which Jesus submitted to (Luke 22:42) ("Father, if it is Your will, take this cup away from Me; nevertheless not My will, but Yours, be done"). Stated differently, the character of Jesus's omniscience is the ability to know all things, but Jesus did not always exercise this ability, just as the nature of Jesus's omnipotence was the power to do all things, even though Jesus did not always exercise this power.

3. Several Verses Appear to Deny Jesus's Omnipotence

If Jesus were God, he would be omnipotent. However, several verses appear to deny His omnipotence. We examine each of these in turn.

a) Verses

(1) Jesus Would Have Relied on the Father to Send Twelve Legions of
    Angels at Gethsemane (Matthew 26)

While Jesus was at Gethsemane with His apostles, Judas came to
Jesus with a great multitude with swords and clubs (Mat 26:47) and
betrayed Jesus (Mat 26:49-50). Peter "stretched out his hand and drew
his sword, struck the servant of the high priest, and cut off his ear" (Mat
26:51). At that moment, Jesus said to him (Mat 26:52-53):

> Put your sword in its place, for all who take the sword will perish by
> the sword. Or do you think that I cannot now pray to My Father, and
> He will provide Me with more than twelve legions of angels?

This verse, which indicates that Jesus would have relied on the
Father to send 12 legions of angels, implies that Jesus could not, on His
own, call up 12 legions of angels to rescue Him. In having relief on the
Father, Jesus evidently did not have the power to call up the angels on
His own.

(2) Jesus Can of Himself Do Nothing; He Relies on the Father's
    Authority (John 5)

John 5 makes clear that Jesus's authority derives from the Father and
Jesus can, of Himself, do nothing (John 5:26-30):

> For as the Father has life in Himself, so He has granted the Son to
> have life in Himself, and has given Him authority to execute
> judgment also, because He is the Son of Man. Do not marvel at this;
> for the hour is coming in which all who are in the graves will hear
> His voice and come forth—those who have done good, to the
> resurrection of life, and those who have done evil, to the
> resurrection of condemnation. I can of Myself do nothing. As I hear,
> I judge; and My judgment is righteous, because I do not seek My
> own will but the will of the Father who sent Me.

b) Response

The fact that Jesus would have relied on the Father to call up 12
legions of angels and that Jesus could of Himself "do nothing" indicates
that Jesus did not have the power to do all things Himself. This certainly
indicates that each member of the Trinity, on His own, does not have all

of the attributes of the triune Godhead. However, it does *not* deny the proposition that the Father, Son and Holy Spirit are each distinct persons having His own attributes and, when joined together, form a triune, omniscient and omnipotent God.

c) *Problem with Response: If Jesus Depends on the Father to Do Anything, then Jesus and the Father Cannot Both Be God*

However, this leads to a different problem. If Jesus is distinct from the Father, and each have their own distinct attributes and powers (*e.g.*, the Father is omnipotent of Himself but Jesus must rely on the Father to do anything), then how can both Jesus and the Father be the same God? In other words, if Jesus is God and the Father is God, then Jesus and the Father must necessarily be the same, but They are not; rather, Jesus is the Son, who depends on the Father to do anything, and the Father is the omnipotent begetter of Jesus.

d) *Answer to Problem with Response*

The problem cited above is in itself problematic because it presumes that just because Jesus and the Father are both God, then both must be identical to one another in every way. In other words, if Jesus is God and the Father is God, then Jesus must be the Father, and identical to Him in every way, and vice versa. Therefore, Jesus cannot depend on the Father for anything as this would imply that Jesus and the Father are not the same (*i.e.*, Jesus cannot be dependent on the Father).

However, the fact that Jesus and the Father are both God does not necessarily mean that they are each identical to one another in every way. Each may have His own distinct attributes, yet still be God. This is because Jesus and the Father are not God in the coterminous sense; rather, they are God in the ontological and metaphysical sense—that is to say, they are God *in essence*.

One can similarly say that water is, in its essence, H_2O, as is ice and steam. Yet water is not *coterminous* with H_2O; it is a manifestation of it. H_2O can take other forms. In the same way, Jesus is God *in essence*, yet He is not identical to God. God is a Trinity; Jesus is the incarnation of God. We can thus conclude that although Jesus and God (as with Jesus and the Father and Jesus and the Holy) are not identical, they are one in essence. Both can be God, and yet Jesus can depend on another Person of the Trinity for strength or in prayer.

B. Jesus Was Not the Alpha and the Omega

1. Overview

Next, Dr. Philips denies that the account in Revelation 1:8 was originally intended to refer to Jesus. He writes (p. 43):

> In the Book of Revelation 1, verse 8, it is implied that Jesus said the following about himself: "I am Alpha and Omega, the beginning and the ending, saith the Lord, which is, and which was, and which is to come, the Almighty." These are the attributes of God. Consequently, Jesus, according to early Christians, is here claiming divinity. However, the above-mentioned wording is according to the King James Version. In the Revised Standard Version, biblical scholars corrected the translation and wrote: "I am the Alpha and the Omega," says the Lord God, who is and who was and who is to come, the Almighty." A correction was also made in the New American Bible produced by Catholics. The translation of that verse has been amended to put it in its correct context as follows: "The Lord God says: I am the Alpha and the Omega, the one who is and who was, and who is to come, the Almighty.'"

2. Response

There are several problems with Dr. Philips' argument. We will discuss each of them herein.

a) The Context Makes It Evident that Jesus Is the Speaker in Revelation 1:8

(1) The Verses Preceding Revelation 1:8 Make It Evident that Jesus Is the Speaker

The verses preceding Revelation 1:8 make evident that Jesus is the speaker in Revelation 1:8. The following verses, which precede Revelation 1:8, are clearly discussing Jesus:

> Rev 1:5 ... Jesus Christ, the faithful witness, the firstborn from the dead, and the ruler over the kings of the earth. To Him who loved us and washed us from our sins in His own blood,

> Rev 1:6 and has made us kings and priests to His God and Father, to Him be glory and dominion forever and ever. Amen.

Rev 1:7 Behold, He is coming with clouds, and every eye will see Him, even they who pierced Him. And all the tribes of the earth will mourn because of Him. Even so, Amen.

(2) The Verses Following Revelation 1:8 Make It Evident that Jesus Is the Speaker

The verses following Revelation 1:8 make it evident that in Revelation 1:8, it is Jesus who refers to himself as the Alpha and Omega, the beginning and the end. John heard a voice that said, "I am the Alpha and the Omega" (Rev 1:11). When John turned, he saw seven golden lampstands (Rev 1:12) and in the midst of them, "One like the Son of Man" (Rev 1:13). The expression "the Son of man" occurs 81 times in the Greek text of the four Gospels, and is used only in the sayings of Jesus. Jesus is referred to as the Son of Man throughout the New Testament. The Trinitarian Godhead is never referred to as the Son of Man in the Bible.

Rev 1:9 I, John, both your brother and companion in the tribulation and kingdom and patience of Jesus Christ, was on the island that is called Patmos for the word of God and for the testimony of Jesus Christ.

Rev 1:10 I was in the Spirit on the Lord's Day, and I heard behind me a loud voice, as of a trumpet,

Rev 1:11 saying, "I am the Alpha and the Omega, the First and the Last," and, "What you see, write in a book and send it to the seven churches which are in Asia: to Ephesus, to Smyrna, to Pergamos, to Thyatira, to Sardis, to Philadelphia, and to Laodicea."

Rev 1:12 Then I turned to see the voice that spoke with me. And having turned I saw seven golden lampstands,

Rev 1:13 and in the midst of the seven lampstands One like the Son of Man, clothed with a garment down to the feet and girded about the chest with a golden band.

Rev 1:14 His head and hair were white like wool, as white as snow, and His eyes like a flame of fire;

Rev 1:15 His feet were like fine brass, as if refined in a furnace, and His voice as the sound of many waters;

Rev 1:16 He had in His right hand seven stars, out of His mouth went a sharp two-edged sword, and His countenance was like the sun shining in its strength.

(3) Verses Further Describing the Speaker in Revelation 1:8 Make It Evident that Jesus Is the Speaker

The verses following Revelation 1:8 further describe the speaker in Revelation 1:8 and make it evident that the speaker can only be Jesus:

- The speaker in Revelation 1:8 had a physical body, for "He laid His right hand on me, saying to me, 'Do not be afraid; I am the First and the Last'" (Rev 1:17). The speaker refers to "My right hand" (Rev 1:20). Jesus is God in the incarnate form of a man. He took on a physical form with a physical body. The Trinitarian Godhead is not incarnate and has no physical body.
- The speaker states that "I am He who lives, and was dead, and behold, I am alive forevermore" (Rev 1:18). Jesus was dead following His crucifixion and came back to life following His resurrection. The Trinitarian Godhead did not die and come back to life.

(4) The Alpha and Omega Gives Water that Forever Quenches Thirst and Thus Must Be Jesus (Revelation 21)

In Revelation 21:6, the speaker says, "I am the Alpha and the Omega, the Beginning and the End. I will give of the fountain of the water of life freely to him who thirsts." These were the words of Jesus in John 4:14, where He said, "whoever drinks of the water that I shall give him will never thirst. But the water that I shall give him will become in him a fountain of water springing up into everlasting life."

(5) The Alpha and Omega Gives to "Every One According to His Work" and Thus Must Be Jesus, Who Judges (Revelation 22)

(a) Overview

Revelation 22 states that the Alpha and Omega gives to "every one according to his work":

Rev 22:12 "And behold, I am coming quickly, and My reward is with Me, to give to every one according to his work.

Rev 22:13 I am the Alpha and the Omega, the Beginning and the End, the First and the Last."

Here we are made keenly aware that the Alpha and Omega is charged with judging mankind. Based on other verses that occur throughout the Bible, we can conclude that the Alpha and Omega is Jesus, who is charged with judging mankind. John 5 makes clear that the Father has granted the Son authority to judge mankind. John states:

John 5:21 For as the Father raises the dead and gives life to them, even so the Son gives life to whom He will.

John 5:22 For the Father judges no one, but *has committed all judgment to the Son*,

John 5:23 that all should honor the Son just as they honor the Father. He who does not honor the Son does not honor the Father who sent Him.

…

John 5:26 For as the Father has life in Himself, so He has granted the Son to have life in Himself,

John 5:27 and *has given Him authority to execute judgment* also, because He is the Son of Man.

John 5:28 Do not marvel at this; for the hour is coming in which all who are in the graves will hear His voice

John 5:29 and come forth—those who have done good, to the resurrection of life, and those who have done evil, to the resurrection of condemnation.

Jesus's judgment is based on the Father's will, but the Father has delegated to Jesus the authority to judge:

John 5:30 I can of Myself do nothing. *As I hear, I judge*; and My judgment is righteous, because I do not seek My own will but the will of the Father who sent Me.

John 5:31 "If I bear witness of Myself, My witness is not true.

It is thus clear that the Alpha and Omega, who is charged with judging mankind, is Jesus.

(b) Verses that State that the Father, Not Jesus, Judges

However, it must be pointed out that some verses in the Bible state that the Father, not Jesus, is the judge. 1 Peter 1 states that the Father judges without partiality according to each one's work:

> 1Pe 1:17 And if you call on the Father, *who without partiality judges according to each one's work*, conduct yourselves throughout the time of your stay here in fear.

This verse must be read in conjunction with John 5:30, which states that when Jesus judges, He seeks the will of the Father. The Father thus judges *through* Jesus, and Jesus judges as the agent of the Father. Acts 17:31 states that God "has appointed a day on which He will judge the world in righteousness by the Man whom He has ordained. He has given assurance of this to all by raising Him from the dead." This indicates that Jesus judges as an agent of God.

The idea of agency, and the imputation of an agent's acts or omissions to his principal, can be found throughout scripture. For example:

> Mat 10:40 "He who receives you receives Me, and he who receives Me receives Him who sent Me.

> Luke 10:16 He who hears you hears Me, he who rejects you rejects Me, and he who rejects Me rejects Him who sent Me."

> John 12:44 Then Jesus cried out and said, "He who believes in Me, believes not in Me but in Him who sent Me. John 12:45 And he who sees Me sees Him who sent Me.

> John 13:20 Most assuredly, I say to you, he who receives whomever I send receives Me; and he who receives Me receives Him who sent Me."

> John 14:9 Jesus said to him, "Have I been with you so long, and yet you have not known Me, Philip? He who has seen Me has seen the Father; so how can you say, 'Show us the Father'? John 14:10 Do you not believe that I am in the Father, and the Father in Me? The words that I speak to you I do not speak on My own authority; but the Father who dwells in Me does the works.

It is thus Jesus who judges, but His judgment is not His own, but the Father's. Thus, when Revelation 22:12 states that "I am coming quickly, and My reward is with Me, to give to every one according to his work," it is referring to Jesus.

(c) The Alpha and Omega is "Coming Quickly"

That Revelation 22:12 is referring to Jesus is further made clear by the statement "I am coming quickly." It is Jesus who will be coming into the world. He will return at His second coming to judge all of mankind:

> Mat 25:31 "When the Son of Man comes in His glory, and all the holy angels with Him, then He will sit on the throne of His glory.
>
> Mat 25:32 All the nations will be gathered before Him, and He will separate them one from another, as a shepherd divides his sheep from the goats.
>
> Mat 25:33 And He will set the sheep on His right hand, but the goats on the left.
>
> Mat 25:34 Then the King will say to those on His right hand, 'Come, you blessed of My Father, inherit the kingdom prepared for you from the foundation of the world:
>
> Mat 25:35 for I was hungry and you gave Me food; I was thirsty and you gave Me drink; I was a stranger and you took Me in;
>
> Mat 25:36 I was naked and you clothed Me; I was sick and you visited Me; I was in prison and you came to Me.'

(6) The Alpha and Omega Self-Identifies As Jesus (Revelation 22)

In case there is any doubt left as to the identification of the Alpha and the Omega, Revelation 22:16 definitively establishes that He is Jesus. Revelation 22:16, which occurs just three verses after verse 22:13's self-identification as the Alpha and Omega, makes clear that He is Jesus:

> Rev 22:16 "I, Jesus, have sent My angel to testify to you these things in the churches. I am the Root and the Offspring of David, the Bright and Morning Star."

As the fifth-to-last verse in the Bible, Revelation 22:16 serves as a final reminder to any reader who, having read the rest of the Bible, has any lingering doubts as to the Bible's message of Jesus's identity as God.

b) *Dr. Philips Assumes that Jesus Cannot Be the Speaker in Revelation 1:8 Because the Verse States that the "Lord" Is the Speaker*

Another error in Dr. Philips' analysis is the assumption that because the verse states that it is the "Lord" who asserts that He is the Alpha and the Omega, that it cannot be Jesus who is speaking. This assumption is based on the faulty premise that Jesus is not "Lord." However, numerous verses in the Scriptures confirm that Jesus is, in fact, Lord. Jesus, being God in essence, is referred to as Lord throughout the New Testament. For example:

- Thomas called out to Jesus as "My Lord and my God!" (John 20:28);
- Elizabeth referred to Jesus as "my Lord" in Luke 1:43 ("why is this granted to me, that the mother of my Lord should come to me?");
- Mary Magdalene referred to Jesus as "my Lord" in John 20:13 ("they have taken away my Lord, and I do not know where they have laid Him").

Therefore, the fact that the verse states that it is the "Lord" who was speaking does not necessarily mean that it cannot be Jesus speaking.

c) *Even If the Verse Were Referring to the Trinitarian God, We Could Still Adduce that Jesus is God from Other Verses*

Even if the verse were referring to the Trinitarian God (as opposed to Jesus), we could still adduce that Jesus is God from other verses throughout the Bible. In other words, Revelation 1:8 is not needed to establish the divinity of Christ because it is just one of many verses that point to divinity. Many other verses establish His divinity. For example:

- Jesus proclaimed to be God before the Sanhedrin:

  Mat 26:63 But Jesus kept silent. And the high priest answered and said to Him, "I put You under oath by the living God: Tell us if You are the Christ, the Son of God!"

  Mat 26:64 Jesus said to him, "It is as you said. Nevertheless, I say to you, hereafter you will see the Son of Man sitting at the right hand of the Power, and coming on the clouds of heaven."

  Mat 26:65 Then the high priest tore his clothes, saying, "He has spoken blasphemy! What further need do we have of witnesses? Look, now you have heard His blasphemy!

- Jesus acknowledged before Pontius Pilate that He was the king of the Jews, but that His kingdom was not of this world. He therefore implied that He was a divine king, which is consistent with His claim of being the Son of God:

John 18:36 Jesus answered, "My kingdom is not of this world. If My kingdom were of this world, My servants would fight, so that I should not be delivered to the Jews; but now My kingdom is not from here."

John 18:37 Pilate therefore said to Him, "Are You a king then?" Jesus answered, "You say rightly that I am a king. For this cause I was born, and for this cause I have come into the world, that I should bear witness to the truth. Everyone who is of the truth hears My voice."

- Rather than deny that He was the son of God or chastise Peter, Jesus praised Peter when Peter confessed that Jesus was "the Christ, the Son of the living God" (Mat 16:16):

Mat 16:15 He said to them, "But who do you say that I am?"

Mat 16:16 Simon Peter answered and said, "You are the Christ, the Son of the living God."

Mat 16:17 Jesus answered and said to him, "Blessed are you, Simon Bar-Jonah, for flesh and blood has not revealed this to you, but My Father who is in heaven.

Dr. Philipps makes no arguments to attempt to prove that these many other verses found throughout the Bible were later additions or corruptions.

C. Jesus's Existence Prior to His Appearance on Earth Is Not Evidence of His Divinity

1. Overview

Dr. Philips writes (p. 42):

Another verse commonly used to support the divinity of Jesus is John 8:58: "Jesus said unto them, 'Verily, verily, I say unto you, Before Abraham was, I am.'" This verse is taken to imply that Jesus existed prior to his appearance on earth. The conclusion drawn from it is that Jesus must be God, since his existence predates his birth on earth. However, the concept of the pre-existence of the prophets, and of man in general, exists in both the Old Testament, as well as in the Qur'aan.

Dr. Philips then cites three examples—Jeremiah, Solomon and Job, which we examine below.

2. Examples

a) Jeremiah 1:4-5

(1) Overview

Dr. Philips writes (p. 42):

> Jeremiah described himself in The Book of Jeremiah 1:4-5 as follows: "Now the word of the Lord came to me saying, 'Before I formed you in the womb I knew you, and before you were born I consecrated you; I appointed you a prophet to the nations.'"

The verses in question are Jeremiah 1:4-5, as follows:

> Jer 1:4 Then the word of the Lord came to me, saying:

> Jer 1:5 "Before I formed you in the womb I knew you; Before you were born I sanctified you; I ordained you a prophet to the nations."

(2) Response

Dr. Philips confuses Jesus's statement, whereby He states that He preexisted Abraham, with Jeremiah's statement, about God's knowledge and ordainment of him as a prophet before he was formed in the womb. Here, there is a fundamental error in Dr. Philip's interpretation of Jeremiah 1:4-5. Jeremiah is not stating that before he was formed in the womb, he existed. Rather, he is stating that before he was formed in the womb, God knew him, sanctified him and ordained him a prophet. This is referring not to Jeremiah's eternity or timelessness, which are exclusive to God alone, nor is it stating that Jeremiah existed prior to being formed in the womb. The statement does not refer to Jeremiah's divinity at all; on the contrary, it refers to God's eternity, and specifically, his omniscience and ability to transcend time. It is not that Jeremiah existed prior to be formed in the womb but rather, before Jeremiah was formed in the womb, God, in his omniscience, knew him, just as He knows all things. Moreover, God, whose omnipotent powers are not limited by time, sanctified and ordained Jeremiah before he was a prophet. Taken together, these verses point to God's nature as omniscient and omnipotent, and His ability to sanctify and ordain things before they even come into existence. Nothing in the verses suggests that Jeremiah existed prior to his being formed in the womb.

b) *Solomon 8:23-27*

Dr. Philips writes:

> Prophet Solomon is reported in Proverbs 8:23-27, to have said, "Ages ago I was set up at the first, before the beginning of the earth. When there were no depths I was brought forth, when there were no springs abounding with water, Before the mountains had been shaped, before the hills, I was brought forth; before he had made the earth with its fields. or the first of the dust of the world When he established the heavens, I was there."

Here, Dr. Philips' error is to confuse the writer of Proverbs, Solomon, with the personification of wisdom, which is quoted in the passage. The text quoted in Proverbs 8 does not constitute the words of Solomon, but rather, the words of wisdom, which addresses mankind. In fact, Solomon quotes the words of wisdom throughout the book of Proverbs. For example, in Proverbs 1:

> Pro 1:20 Wisdom calls aloud outside; She raises her voice in the open squares.

> Pro 1:21 She cries out in the chief concourses, At the openings of the gates in the city She speaks her words;

> Pro 1:22 "How long, you simple ones, will you love simplicity? For scorners delight in their scorning, And fools hate knowledge.

> …

> Pro 1:33 But whoever listens to me will dwell safely, And will be secure, without fear of evil."

Similarly, in Proverbs 9, wisdom speaks:

> Pro 9:1 Wisdom has built her house, She has hewn out her seven pillars;

> …

> Pro 9:3 She has sent out her maidens, She cries out from the highest places of the city,

Pro 9:4 "Whoever is simple, let him turn in here!" As for him who lacks understanding, she says to him,

Pro 9:5 "Come, eat of my bread And drink of the wine I have mixed.

Pro 9:6 Forsake foolishness and live, And go in the way of understanding."

Wisdom's speech addressing mankind is placed in quotation marks to distinguish it from the speech of Solomon. The words "Listen, for I will speak of excellent things, And from the opening of my lips will come right things" in Proverbs 8:6 are not Solomon's words, but the words of wisdom, which Solomon is quoting. Therefore, while Solomon is the prophet and the scribe of Proverbs, the words of Proverbs 8:23-27 are to be attributed to wisdom. If Dr. Philips read the beginning of the passage, at Proverbs 8:12, he would have seen that it is wisdom that is speaking:

Pro 8:12 "I, wisdom, dwell with prudence, And find out knowledge and discretion."

Therefore, it is not Solomon who is existed when God "established the clouds above, When He strengthened the fountains of the deep" (Pro 8:28); rather, it is wisdom. It was not Solomon who was beside God when he "assigned to the sea its limit, So that the waters would not transgress His command, When He marked out the foundations of the earth" (Pro 8:29); rather, it was wisdom.

Similarly, it is not Solomon who, if anyone finds him, "obtains favor from the Lord" (Pro 8:35); rather, it is wisdom. In this same manner, it is not Solomon who, if anyone sins against him, "wrongs his own soul" (Pro 8:36) and who, if anyone hates him, "loves death" (Pro 8:36); rather, it is wisdom. The passages therefore do not refer to the timelessness of Solomon but of wisdom.

c) Job

(1) Overview

Next, Dr. Philips writes (p. 44-45):

According to Job 38:4 and 21, God addresses Prophet Job as follows: "Where were you when I laid the foundation of the earth?

Tell me, if you have understanding ... You Know, for you were born then, and the number of your days is great!"

(2) Response

(a) Overview: God is Questioning Job and Using Sarcasm

Dr. Philips again enters into a fundamental error of biblical interpretation. He fails to consider Job 38:3, the verse just before the passage that he quotes, which makes it clear that the passage that follows consists of a questioning of Job. Job 38:3 states, "Now prepare yourself like a man; I will question you, and you shall answer Me." What follows is a passage that speaks of God's glory, omnipotence and the wonders of the world that God created. Much of God's words involves sarcastic asides that point to man's inferiority to God. Among these passages is Job 38:21, which states:

> Job 38:21 Do you know it, because you were born then, Or because the number of your days is great?

Here, God is not implying that Job was actually born when God laid the foundations of the earth. He is in fact utilizing sarcasm to state that Job was not present at that time. In fact, man had not yet even been created until the sixth day, after God had laid the foundations of the world on days one through four, according to the Genesis creation account. Yet even if God had created man on day one, He would have created Adam, a forefather of Job that lived thousands of years earlier. To interpret Job 38 as Dr. Philips suggests would be wholly incompatible with the Genesis account of the creation. The author of both Genesis and Job was most likely Moses, and Moses would not have so egregiously contradicted himself.

(b) Although No Question Mark Is Used in the Hebrew, It Is Clear that Job is Being Questioned

The original Hebrew of Job 38 does *not* use question marks throughout the passage. Moreover, certain translations of Job 38:21 do not phrase the sentence as a question. Examples abound:

Version	Verse	Statem.	Ques.
ESV	You know, for you were born then, and the number of your days is great!	✓	☒

ASV	Doubtless, thou knowest, for thou wast then born, And the number of thy days is great!	✓	☒
NIV	Surely you know, for you were already born! You have lived so many years!	✓	☒
KJV	Knowest thou it, because thou wast then born? or because the number of thy days is great?	☒	✓
NKJV	Do you know it, because you were born then, Or because the number of your days is great?	☒	✓

Regardless of how the verse has been translated, the context makes clear that the entire passage consists of God's questioning of Job. This is explicitly stated in Job 38:3:

> Now prepare yourself like a man; I will question you, and you shall answer Me.

Given the context, the text of Job 38:3 and the Genesis account of creation, which states that God had not formed man until the sixth day, it is best to read Job 38:21 as sublime irony. Benson's Commentary characterizes Job 38:38:21 as an "ironical question" and notes:

> If thou pretendest that thou knowest these things, how camest thou by this knowledge? Was it because thou didst then exist in the full and perfect use of thy faculties, and thereby hadst the opportunity of inspecting my works, and of seeing whence the light came? Or, because thou hast gained this knowledge by long experience, as having lived ever since the creation of the world until this time? Whereas, in truth, thou art but of yesterday, and knowest, comparatively, nothing, Job 8:9.

D. Being Called "Son of God" Is Not Evidence of Jesus's Divinity because Others Had This Title and because Jesus Denied Being the Son of God

1. Overview

a)   Others Had the Title "Son of God"

Dr. Philips argues that the title "son of God" is not evidence of Jesus's divinity because the term is used throughout the Bible to refer to other individuals who did not hold divinity. Specifically, Dr. Philips writes (p. 45-48):

> Another of the evidences used for Jesus' divinity is the application of the title "Son of God" to Jesus. However, there are numerous places in the Old Testament where this title has been given to others.

> God called Israel (Prophet Jacob) His "son" when He instructed Prophet Moses to go to Pharaoh in Exodus 4:22-23, "And you shall say to Pharaoh, 'Thus says the Lord, 'Israel is my first-born son, and I say to you, 'Let my son go that he may serve me.'"

> In 2nd Samuel 8:13-14 [sic; this should cite to 2Sa 7:13-14], God calls Prophet Solomon His son, "He [Solomon] shall build a house for my name, and I will establish the throne of his kingdom forever. I will be his father, and he shall be my son."

> God promised to make Prophet David His son in Psalms 89:26-27: "He shall cry unto me, 'Thou art my father, my God, and the rock of my salvation,' Also I will make him my first-born, higher than the kings of the earth."

> Angels are referred to as "sons of God" in The Book of Job 1:6, "Now there was a day when the sons of God came to present themselves before the Lord, and Satan also came among them."

> In the New Testament, there are many references to "sons of God" other than Jesus. For example, when the author of the Gospel according to Luke listed Jesus' ancestors back to Adam, he wrote: "The son of Enos, the son of Seth, the son of Adam, the son of God."

> Some claim that what is unique in the case of Jesus, is that he is the only begotten Son of God, while the others are merely "sons of God". However, God is recorded as saying to Prophet David, in Psalms 2:7, "I will tell the decree of the Lord: He said to me, 'You are my son, today I have begotten you.'"

b)   Jesus Denied Being the Son of God

Dr. Philips further argues that Jesus denied being the Son of God (p. 47-48):

> It should also be noted that nowhere in the Gospels does Jesus actually call himself "Son of God". Instead, he is recorded to have repeatedly called himself "Son of man" (e.g. Luke 9:22) innumerable times. And in Luke 4:41, he actually rejected being called "Son of God": "And demons also came out of many, crying, 'You are the Son of God!' But he rebuked them, and would not allow them to speak, because they knew that he was the Christ."

2.   References to the "Son of God' Are References to Jesus

As we will see herein, references to the "Son of God" in the Bible are references to Jesus. This title is given to Jesus by Satan, demons, the apostles and disciples, the Sanhedrin and Pontius Pilate. In these instances, Jesus never denies or refuses the title. Instead, he *acknowledges* being the Son of God in front of Peter, the Sanhedrin and Pontius Pilate.

a)   Introduction

By studying the versions that refer to "the Son of God" in the Bible, we learn that these references are to Jesus, who never denies the title.

b)   General References to Jesus as "the Son of God"

(1) Daniel 3: The Son of God in the Fiery Furnace

In Daniel, after King Nebuchadnezzar cast Shadrach, Meshach, and Abed-Nego into the fiery furnace, he witnessed a fourth in the furnace in the form of the Son of God:

> Dan 3:24 Then King Nebuchadnezzar was astonished; and he rose in haste and spoke, saying to his counselors, "Did we not cast three men bound into the midst of the fire?" They answered and said to the king, "True, O king."

> Dan 3:25 "Look!" he answered, "I see four men loose, walking in the midst of the fire; and they are not hurt, and the form of the fourth is like the Son of God."

(2) Matthew 27, Mark 15: The Centurion Declares Jesus to Be the Son of God after the Earthquake

After Jesus died on the cross, the veil of the temple was torn in two from top to bottom; and the earth quaked, the rocks were split, the graves were opened and bodies of the saints were raised from the dead and appeared to many (Mat 27:51-53). Following these extraordinary signs and wonders, the centurion and those with him declared that Jesus was the Son of God:

> Mat 27:54 So when the centurion and those with him, who were guarding Jesus, saw the earthquake and the things that had happened, they feared greatly, saying, "Truly this was the Son of God!"

Mark gives a similar account:

> Mark 15:37 And Jesus cried out with a loud voice, and breathed His last.

> Mark 15:38 Then the veil of the temple was torn in two from top to bottom.

> Mark 15:39 So when the centurion, who stood opposite Him, saw that He cried out like this and breathed His last, he said, "Truly this Man was the Son of God!"

(3) Luke 1: The Angel Gabriel Declared that Mary Would Give Birth to the Son of God

In the Gospel of Luke, the angel Gabriel declared to Mary that she would give birth to the Son of God:

> Luke 1:26 Now in the sixth month the angel Gabriel was sent by God to a city of Galilee named Nazareth,
>
> ...
>
> Luke 1:35 And the angel answered and said to her, "The Holy Spirit will come upon you, and the power of the Highest will overshadow you; therefore, also, that Holy One who is to be born will be called the Son of God.

c) Jesus Acknowledged that He Was the Son of God

(1) Matthew 16: Jesus Praised Peter for Calling Him the Son of God

Rather than deny that He was the Son of God or chastise Peter, Jesus praised Peter when Peter confessed that Jesus was "the Christ, the Son of the living God" (Mat 16:16):

> Mat 16:15 He said to them, "But who do you say that I am?"

> Mat 16:16 Simon Peter answered and said, "You are the Christ, the Son of the living God."

> Mat 16:17 Jesus answered and said to him, "Blessed are you, Simon Bar-Jonah, for flesh and blood has not revealed this to you, but My Father who is in heaven.

(2) Matthew 26, Luke 22: Jesus Proclaimed before the Sanhedrin to be the Son of God

Jesus proclaimed to be God before the Sanhedrin:

> Mat 26:63 But Jesus kept silent. And the high priest answered and said to Him, "I put You under oath by the living God: Tell us if You are the Christ, the Son of God!"

> Mat 26:64 Jesus said to him, "It is as you said. Nevertheless, I say to you, hereafter you will see the Son of Man sitting at the right hand of the Power, and coming on the clouds of heaven."

> Mat 26:65 Then the high priest tore his clothes, saying, "He has spoken blasphemy! What further need do we have of witnesses? Look, now you have heard His blasphemy!

Luke gives a similar account:

> Luke 22:70 Then they all said, "Are You then the Son of God?" So He said to them, "You rightly say that I am."

> Luke 22:71 And they said, "What further testimony do we need? For we have heard it ourselves from His own mouth."

(3) Matthew 27: Jesus Said "I am the Son of God"

Mathew writes:

Mat 27:39 And those who passed by blasphemed Him, wagging their heads

Mat 27:40 and saying, "You who destroy the temple and build it in three days, save Yourself! If You are the Son of God, come down from the cross."

Mat 27:41 Likewise the chief priests also, mocking with the scribes and elders, said,

Mat 27:42 "He saved others; Himself He cannot save. If He is the King of Israel, let Him now come down from the cross, and we will believe Him.

Mat 27:43 He trusted in God; let Him deliver Him now if He will have Him; for He said, 'I am the Son of God.'"

In Matthew 27, passersby blasphemed Jesus as he hung on the cross, declaring, "If You are the Son of God, come down from the cross" (Mat 27:40). These passersby did not make up the idea that Jesus was the Son of God out of thin air. Like the apostles, the Sanhedrin, the demons and Pontius Pilate, they adduced this claim, and their indirect challenge of Jesus, from Jesus's own claim to be the Son of God. As recounted in Mark, the chief priests said, "He trusted in God; let Him deliver Him now if He will have Him; for He said, 'I am the Son of God.'"

(4) John 3: Jesus Declared to Nicodemus that He Was the Son of God

Jesus said to Nicodemus that "God so loved the world that He gave His only begotten Son, that whoever believes in Him should not perish but have everlasting life. For God did not send His Son into the world to condemn the world, but that the world through Him might be saved. He who believes in Him is not condemned; but he who does not believe is condemned already, because he has not believed in the name of the only begotten Son of God" (John 3:16-18). This son of God was none other than Jesus, who came into the world to save it. The passage is as follows:

John 3:10 Jesus answered and said to him, "Are you the teacher of Israel, and do not know these things?

John 3:11 Most assuredly, I say to you, We speak what We know and testify what We have seen, and you do not receive Our witness.

John 3:12 If I have told you earthly things and you do not believe, how will you believe if I tell you heavenly things?

John 3:13 No one has ascended to heaven but He who came down from heaven, that is, the Son of Man who is in heaven.

John 3:14 And as Moses lifted up the serpent in the wilderness, even so must the Son of Man be lifted up,

John 3:15 that whoever believes in Him should not perish but have eternal life.

John 3:16 For God so loved the world that He gave His only begotten Son, that whoever believes in Him should not perish but have everlasting life.

John 3:17 For God did not send His Son into the world to condemn the world, but that the world through Him might be saved.

John 3:18 "He who believes in Him is not condemned; but he who does not believe is condemned already, because he has not believed in the name of the only begotten Son of God."

(5) John 5: Jesus Declares He Is the Son of God and All Who Hear His Word Will Live

Jesus again declares that He is the Son of God, declaring that "he who hears My word and believes in Him who sent Me has everlasting life, and shall not come into judgment ... the hour is coming, and now is, when the dead will hear the voice of the Son of God; and those who hear will live" (John 5:24-25). Here, He is equating those who hear Jesus's word with those who hear the voice of the Son of God. The two groups are thus the same, and both have eternal life. The passage is as follows:

John 5:24 "Most assuredly, I say to you, he who hears My word and believes in Him who sent Me has everlasting life, and shall not come into judgment, but has passed from death into life.

John 5:25 Most assuredly, I say to you, the hour is coming, and now is, when the dead will hear the voice of the Son of God; and those who hear will live.

John 5:26 For as the Father has life in Himself, so He has granted the Son to have life in Himself,

John 5:27 and has given Him authority to execute judgment also, because He is the Son of Man.

John 5:28 Do not marvel at this; for the hour is coming in which all who are in the graves will hear His voice

John 5:29 and come forth—those who have done good, to the resurrection of life, and those who have done evil, to the resurrection of condemnation.

John 5:30 I can of Myself do nothing. As I hear, I judge; and My judgment is righteous, because I do not seek My own will but the will of the Father who sent Me.

(6) John 9: Jesus Declared to the Blind Man He was the Son of God

After Jesus healed the blind man, the Pharisees accused Him of breaking the Sabbath. They then questioned the blind man's parents because they did not believe that he had been blind. The parents told the Jews to ask the man who had been born blind. The man replied that he did not know whether Jesus was a sinner, but he knew that although he was born blind, he could now see (John 9:25). The man then declared that if Jesus was not from God, that he could do nothing (John 9:33). The Jews then cast him out (John 9:34). John then gives an account of the man's encounter with Jesus, where he declared that he believed in Jesus, the Son of God:

John 9:35 Jesus heard that they had cast him out; and when He had found him, He said to him, "Do you believe in the Son of God?"

John 9:36 He answered and said, "Who is He, Lord, that I may believe in Him?"

John 9:37 And Jesus said to him, "You have both seen Him and it is He who is talking with you."

John 9:38 Then he said, "Lord, I believe!" And he worshiped Him.

John 9:39 And Jesus said, "For judgment I have come into this world, that those who do not see may see, and that those who see may be made blind."

(7) John 10: Jesus Admits that He Declared Himself to Be the Son of God

After Jesus stated, "I and My Father are one" (John 10:30), the Jews sought to stone Him (John 10:31). In a conversation that followed, Jesus stated that He previously declared, "I am the Son of God" (John 10:36):

John 10:34 Jesus answered them, "Is it not written in your law, 'I SAID, "YOU ARE GODS" '?

John 10:35 If He called them gods, to whom the word of God came (and the Scripture cannot be broken),

John 10:36 do you say of Him whom the Father sanctified and sent into the world, 'You are blaspheming,' because I said, 'I am the Son of God'?

(8) John 18: Jesus Acknowledged before Pilate that He was a Heavenly King

Jesus acknowledged before Pontius Pilate that He was the king of the Jews, but that His kingdom was not of this world. He therefore implied that He was a divine king, which is consistent with His claim of being the Son of God:

John 18:36 Jesus answered, "My kingdom is not of this world. If My kingdom were of this world, My servants would fight, so that I should not be delivered to the Jews; but now My kingdom is not from here."

John 18:37 Pilate therefore said to Him, "Are You a king then?" Jesus answered, "You say rightly that I am a king. For this cause I was born, and for this cause I have come into the world, that I should bear witness to the truth. Everyone who is of the truth hears My voice."

(9) John 19: The Jews Accused Jesus of Calling Himself the Son of God

John 19:5 Then Jesus came out, wearing the crown of thorns and the purple robe. And Pilate said to them, "Behold the Man!"

John 19:6 Therefore, when the chief priests and officers saw Him, they cried out, saying, "Crucify Him, crucify Him!" Pilate said to them, "You take Him and crucify Him, for I find no fault in Him."

John 19:7 The Jews answered him, "We have a law, and according to our law He ought to die, because He made Himself the Son of God."

John 19:8 Therefore, when Pilate heard that saying, he was the more afraid,

d)   The Apostles and Disciples Refer to Jesus as "Son of God"

(1) Matthew 14: The Apostles Declared that Jesus Was the Son of God after Peter Walked on the Water

After Peter walked on the water, the apostles declared that Jesus was the Son of God. Again, there is no indication that Jesus rejected this title:

> Mat 14:29 So He said, "Come." And when Peter had come down out of the boat, he walked on the water to go to Jesus.

> Mat 14:30 But when he saw that the wind was boisterous, he was afraid; and beginning to sink he cried out, saying, "Lord, save me!"

> Mat 14:31 And immediately Jesus stretched out His hand and caught him, and said to him, "O you of little faith, why did you doubt?"

> Mat 14:32 And when they got into the boat, the wind ceased.

> Mat 14:33 Then those who were in the boat came and worshiped Him, saying, "Truly You are the Son of God."

> Mat 14:34 When they had crossed over, they came to the land of Gennesaret.

> Mat 14:35 And when the men of that place recognized Him, they sent out into all that surrounding region, brought to Him all who were sick,

> Mat 14:36 and begged Him that they might only touch the hem of His garment. And as many as touched it were made perfectly well.

(2) Mark 1: Mark Declares Jesus to Be the Son of God

Mark opens his Gospel stating:

> Mark 1:1 The beginning of the gospel of Jesus Christ, the Son of God.

(3) John 1: John the Baptist Testified that Jesus Was the Son of God

John the Baptist testified that Jesus was the Son of God:

> John 1:32 And John bore witness, saying, "I saw the Spirit descending from heaven like a dove, and He remained upon Him.

John 1:33 I did not know Him, but He who sent me to baptize with water said to me, 'Upon whom you see the Spirit descending, and remaining on Him, this is He who baptizes with the Holy Spirit.'

John 1:34 And I have seen and testified that this is the Son of God."

(4) John 1: Nathanael Declared Jesus to Be the Son of God

John 1:49 Nathanael answered and said to Him, "Rabbi, You are the Son of God! You are the King of Israel!"

John 1:50 Jesus answered and said to him, "Because I said to you, 'I saw you under the fig tree,' do you believe? You will see greater things than these."

John 1:51 And He said to him, "Most assuredly, I say to you, hereafter you shall see heaven open, and the angels of God ascending and descending upon the Son of Man."

(5) John 6: Peter Declared that Jesus is the Son of God

Peter declared that Jesus is the "Son of the living God":

John 6:68 But Simon Peter answered Him, "Lord, to whom shall we go? You have the words of eternal life.

John 6:69 Also we have come to believe and know that You are the Christ, the Son of the living God."

(6) John 11: Martha Declared Jesus to Be the Son of God

When Lazarus of Bethany fell sick, his sisters Mary and Martha sent to Jesus to inform Him (John 11:1-3). When Jesus heard this, He left for Judea (John 11:7). Lazarus had died (John 11:14) and had been in the tomb four days when Jesus arrived (John 11:17). Martha said to Jesus that if He had been there, Lazarus would not have died (John 11:21). Jesus replied that He was the resurrection and the life (John 11:25). To this Martha replied that Jesus was the Son of God (John 11:27):

John 11:27 She said to Him, "Yes, Lord, I believe that You are the Christ, the Son of God, who is to come into the world."

Jesus then raised Lazarus from the dead:

John 11:43 Now when He had said these things, He cried with a loud voice, "Lazarus, come forth!"

John 11:44 And he who had died came out bound hand and foot with graveclothes, and his face was wrapped with a cloth. Jesus said to them, "Loose him, and let him go."

(7) John 20: The Apostle John Declares Jesus to Be the Son of God

John 20:31 but these are written that you may believe that Jesus is the Christ, the Son of God, and that believing you may have life in His name.

(8) Acts 35: The Ethiopian Eunuch Declared Jesus to Be the Son of God

Philip encountered an Ethiopian eunuch sitting in a chariot reading Isaiah the prophet (Acts 8:28) and preached Jesus to him (Acts 8:35). The eunuch asked to be baptized and declared his faith that Jesus was the Son of God

Acts 8:35 Then Philip opened his mouth, and beginning at this Scripture, preached Jesus to him.

Acts 8:36 Now as they went down the road, they came to some water. And the eunuch said, "See, here is water. What hinders me from being baptized?"

Acts 8:37 Then Philip said, "If you believe with all your heart, you may." And he answered and said, "I believe that Jesus Christ is the Son of God."

e) *Satan and the Demons Declared Jesus to Be the "Son of God"*

(1) Mathew 4 and Luke 4: When Tempting Jesus, Satan Refers to Jesus as the Son of God

(a) Turning Stones into Bread

In the temptation of Christ, Satan twice referred to Jesus as the Son of God. In both instances, Jesus did not deny being the Son of God. In the first instance, Jesus refused to command stones to become bread, for man does not live by bread alone:

Mat 4:3 Now when the tempter came to Him, he said, "If You are the Son of God, command that these stones become bread."

Mat 4:4 But He answered and said, "It is written, 'MAN SHALL NOT LIVE BY BREAD ALONE, BUT BY EVERY WORD THAT PROCEEDS FROM THE MOUTH OF GOD.' "

Luke gives a similar account:

Luke 4:3 And the devil said to Him, "If You are the Son of God, command this stone to become bread."

Luke 4:4 But Jesus answered him, saying, "It is written, 'MAN SHALL NOT LIVE BY BREAD ALONE, BUT BY EVERY WORD OF GOD.' "

(b) Tempting God

In the second instance, Satan tempted Jesus to tempt God by throwing Himself off of the pinnacle of the temple. Jesus refused to tempt God:

Mat 4:5 Then the devil took Him up into the holy city, set Him on the pinnacle of the temple,

Mat 4:6 and said to Him, "If You are the Son of God, throw Yourself down. For it is written: 'HE SHALL GIVE HIS ANGELS CHARGE OVER YOU,' and, IN THEIR HANDS THEY SHALL BEAR YOU UP, LEST YOU DASH YOUR FOOT AGAINST A STONE.' "

Mat 4:7 Jesus said to him, "It is written again, 'YOU SHALL NOT TEMPT THE Lord YOUR GOD.' "

Luke gives a similar account:

Luke 4:9 Then he brought Him to Jerusalem, set Him on the pinnacle of the temple, and said to Him, "If You are the Son of God, throw Yourself down from here.

Luke 4:10 For it is written: 'HE SHALL GIVE HIS ANGELS CHARGE OVER YOU, TO KEEP YOU,'

Luke 4:11 and, 'IN THEIR HANDS THEY SHALL BEAR YOU UP, LEST YOU DASH YOUR FOOT AGAINST A STONE.' "

Luke 4:12 And Jesus answered and said to him, "It has been said, 'YOU SHALL NOT TEMPT THE Lord YOUR GOD.' "

In these instances, Jesus could have told Satan that He was not, in fact, the Son of God. Instead, He said nothing about his divine nature as God's Son and instead rebuked Satan for his temptations.

(2) Matthew 8: Two Demon-Possessed Men Refer to Jesus as the Son of God

> Mat 8:28 When He had come to the other side, to the country of the Gergesenes, there met Him two demon-possessed men, coming out of the tombs, exceedingly fierce, so that no one could pass that way.
>
> Mat 8:29 And suddenly they cried out, saying, "What have we to do with You, Jesus, You Son of God? Have You come here to torment us before the time?"
>
> Mat 8:30 Now a good way off from them there was a herd of many swine feeding.
>
> Mat 8:31 So the demons begged Him, saying, "If You cast us out, permit us to go away into the herd of swine."
>
> Mat 8:32 And He said to them, "Go." So when they had come out, they went into the herd of swine. And suddenly the whole herd of swine ran violently down the steep place into the sea, and perished in the water.

(3) Mark 3: The Unclean Spirits Declare Jesus to be the Son of God

Mark writes:

> Mark 3:11 And the unclean spirits, whenever they saw Him, fell down before Him and cried out, saying, "You are the Son of God."
>
> Mark 3:12 But He sternly warned them that they should not make Him known.

When the unclean spirits declare Jesus to be the Son of God, Jesus's reaction was *not* to silence them because their declarations are mistaken or wrong. Rather, it was to silence them because at that stage in His ministry, Jesus did not yet want to be made known. By stating that Jesus silenced the unclean spirits because He did not want to be made known, Mark makes clear that Jesus acknowledged being the Son of God (*i.e.*, because the unclean spirits knew who He was and He did not yet want this to be made known).

(4) Mark 5: The Demon Legion Called Jesus "Son of the Most High God"

In Mark 5, the demon Legion called Jesus "Son of the Most High God." Jesus did not deny the title:

> Mark 5:7 And he cried out with a loud voice and said, "What have I to do with You, Jesus, Son of the Most High God? I implore You by God that You do not torment me."
>
> Mark 5:8 For He said to him, "Come out of the man, unclean spirit!"
>
> Mark 5:9 Then He asked him, "What is your name?" And he answered, saying, "My name is Legion; for we are many."
>
> Mark 5:10 Also he begged Him earnestly that He would not send them out of the country.
>
> Mark 5:11 Now a large herd of swine was feeding there near the mountains.
>
> Mark 5:12 So all the demons begged Him, saying, "Send us to the swine, that we may enter them."
>
> Mark 5:13 And at once Jesus gave them permission. Then the unclean spirits went out and entered the swine (there were about two thousand); and the herd ran violently down the steep place into the sea, and drowned in the sea.

(5) Luke 4: Demons Called Jesus "the Son of God"

> Luke 4:41 And demons also came out of many, crying out and saying, "You are the Christ, the Son of God!" And He, rebuking them, did not allow them to speak, for they knew that He was the Christ.

3. Examination of References to Others as "son of God" (Singular)

a) Exodus 4: Israel (Jacob)

(1) Overview

Dr. Philips writes (p. 46):

God called Israel (Prophet Jacob) His "son" when He instructed Prophet Moses to go to Pharaoh in Exodus 4:22-23, "And you shall say to Pharaoh, 'Thus says the Lord, 'Israel is my first-born son, and I say to you, 'Let my son go that he may serve me.'"

The NKJV translates Exodus 4:22-23 as follows:

Exo 4:22 Then you shall say to Pharaoh, 'Thus says the Lord: "Israel is My son, My firstborn.

Exo 4:23 So I say to you, let My son go that he may serve Me. But if you refuse to let him go, indeed I will kill your son, your firstborn." ' "

(2) Response

Exodus 4:22-23 is using the word "son" in a figurative, rather than literal, sense. By the time the genealogy of Israel (Jacob) had reached Moses, Israel had already deceased. Therefore, when Moses states "let My son go," he is not referring to Jacob, who had long since deceased. Rather, he is using "Israel" to refer to all of the people of Israel, including the twelve tribes of Israel (Judah, Levi, Simeon, Reuben, etc.). In other words, Moses is asking Pharaoh to release all of the people of Israel, not the individual Jacob (Israel) who had died generations earlier. If the word "son," when used in Exodus 4:22, is interpreted literally, then the phrase, "let My son go that he may serve Me" (Exo 4:23) is rendered meaningless.

b) 2 Samuel 7: King Solomon

(1) Overview

Dr. Philips writes (p. 46):

In 2nd Samuel 8:13-14 [sic; this should reference 2Sa 7:13-14], God calls Prophet Solomon His son, "He [Solomon] shall build a house for my name, and I will establish the throne of his kingdom forever. I will be his father, and he shall be my son."

(2) Response

In 2 Samuel 7, God instructs Nathan to speak the following to David:

2Sa 7:12 "When your days are fulfilled and you rest with your fathers, I will set up your seed after you, who will come from your body, and I will establish his kingdom.

2Sa 7:13 He shall build a house for My name, and I will establish the throne of his kingdom forever.

2Sa 7:14 I will be his Father, and he shall be My son. If he commits iniquity, I will chasten him with the rod of men and with the blows of the sons of men.

2Sa 7:15 But My mercy shall not depart from him, as I took it from Saul, whom I removed from before you.

2Sa 7:16 And your house and your kingdom shall be established forever before you. Your throne shall be established forever." ' "

2Sa 7:17 According to all these words and according to all this vision, so Nathan spoke to David.

2Sa 7:18 Then King David went in and sat before the Lord; and he said: "Who am I, O Lord GOD? And what is my house, that You have brought me this far?

God states that He will "set up your seed after you, who will come from your body" (2Sa 7:12). The phrase "will come from your body" clearly denotes that the seed will be David's son by blood, and David would be his father.

God then states, "I will be his Father, and he shall be My son" (2Sa 7:14). Here, God is speaking figuratively. We know that David's son could not literally be God's son because, just two verses earlier, God made it clear that David's son would come from David's own body. Therefore, in 2 Samuel 7:14, God was speaking figuratively. Specifically, He meant that David's son would be God's son in the sense that if David's son "commits iniquity, [God] will chasten him with the rod of men and with the blows of the sons of men" (2Sa 7:14). However, God promises that "My mercy shall not depart from him, as I took it from Saul, whom I removed from before you" (2Sa 7:15).

c) *Psalm 2: King David*

(1) Overview

Dr. Philips writes (p. 46):

> Some claim that what is unique in the case of Jesus, is that he is the only begotten Son of God, while the others are merely "sons of God". However, God is recorded as saying to Prophet David, in Psalms 2:7, "I will tell the decree of the Lord: He said to me, 'You are my son, today I have begotten you.'"

(2) Response

Psalm 2 states:

> Psa 2:5 Then He shall speak to them in His wrath, And distress them in His deep displeasure:

> Psa 2:6 "Yet I have set My King On My holy hill of Zion."

> Psa 2:7 "I will declare the decree: The Lord has said to Me, 'You are My Son, Today I have begotten You.

> Psa 2:8 Ask of Me, and I will give You The nations for Your inheritance, And the ends of the earth for Your possession.

> Psa 2:9 You shall break them with a rod of iron; You shall dash them to pieces like a potter's vessel.' "

Here, the Scripture is again referring to a son of God in a figurative, or spiritual sense. God is not David's natural father; the Scripture makes clear that David's natural father was Jesse (Ruth 4:17).

d) Psalm 89: King David

(1) Overview

Dr. Philips writes (p. 47):

> God promised to make Prophet David His son in Psalms 89:26-27: "He shall cry unto me, 'Thou art my father, my God, and the rock of my salvation,' Also I will make him my first-born, higher than the kings of the earth."

(2) Response

Psalm 89 states:

> Psa 89:25 Also I will set his hand over the sea, And his right hand over the rivers.

Psa 89:26 He shall cry to Me, 'You are my Father, My God, and the rock of my salvation.'

Psa 89:27 Also I will make him My firstborn, The highest of the kings of the earth.

Psa 89:28 My mercy I will keep for him forever, And My covenant shall stand firm with him.

Again, the Psalm is not to be interpreted literally. David's natural father was Jesse, so by "firstborn," he is being referred to as a spiritual son of God.

e) Luke 3: Adam is the "Son of God"

(1) Overview

Dr. Philips writes (p. 46-47):

In the New Testament, there are many references to "sons of God" other than Jesus. For example, when the author of the Gospel according to Luke listed Jesus' ancestors back to Adam, he wrote: "The son of Enos, the son of Seth, the son of Adam, the son of God."

The NKJV refers to Adam as the "son of God" (lowercase "s") and translates Luke 3:38 as follows:

Luke 3:38 the son of Enosh, the son of Seth, the son of Adam, the son of God.

(2) Response

Here, Adam's characterization as the son of God can be distinguished from Jesus's characterization as the Son of God. In Luke 3:38, the Evangelist is referring to Adam's genealogy. Therefore, Adam is a "son" of God in the sense that he was created by God (i.e., he had no natural father). Jesus is also the Son of God in the sense that He had no natural father, but in addition, He is the Son of God in a *divine* sense, in that Jesus is a member of the Trinity, along with the Father and the Holy Spirit, and begotten of the Father. Jesus's divine substance is one with that of the Father and the Holy Spirit. It is in this sense that Jesus declared in John 10:30, "I and My Father are one."

4.   Examination of References to "sons of God" (Plural)

a) Overview: Job 1: Angels

Dr. Philips writes (p. 46):

> Angels are referred to as "sons of God" in The Book of Job 1:6, "Now there was a day when the sons of God came to present themselves before the Lord, and Satan also came among them."

b) All References to "sons of God" in the Bible

(1) Genesis 6: The sons of God Took the Daughters of Men as Wives

> Gen 6:1 Now it came to pass, when *men began to multiply on the face of the earth*, and daughters were born to them,

> Gen 6:2 that the *sons of God saw the daughters of men*, that they were beautiful; and they *took wives for themselves of all whom they chose*.

> Gen 6:3 And the Lord said, "My Spirit shall not strive with man forever, for he is indeed flesh; yet his days shall be one hundred and twenty years."

> Gen 6:4 There were giants on the earth in those days, and also afterward, *when the sons of God came in to the daughters of men and they bore children to them*. Those were the mighty men who were of old, men of renown.

> Gen 6:5 Then the Lord saw that the wickedness of man was great in the earth, and that every intent of the thoughts of his heart was only evil continually.

> Gen 6:6 And the Lord was sorry that He had made man on the earth, and He was grieved in His heart.

> Gen 6:7 So the Lord said, "I will destroy man whom I have created from the face of the earth, both man and beast, creeping thing and birds of the air, for I am sorry that I have made them."

> Gen 6:8 But Noah found grace in the eyes of the Lord.

We read here that the sons of God saw the daughters of men and took them as wives. It appears that the sons of God are righteous men, whereas the daughters of men are unrighteous women. This would be consistent with the New Covenant principle that we become sons and daughters of God when we receive Him. For example, John 1 refers to those who receive God has his "children":

> John 1:12 But as many as received Him, to them He gave the right to become children of God, to those who believe in His name:

> John 1:13 who were born, not of blood, nor of the will of the flesh, nor of the will of man, but of God.

Specifically, John distinguishes those who are born of the flesh (*i.e.*, the natural sons and daughters of man) with those who are born of God (*i.e.*, the spiritual sons and daughters of God). Jesus distinguished between those who are born of the flesh and those who are born of the spirit. He stated, "That which is born of the flesh is flesh, and that which is born of the Spirit is spirit" (John 3:6).

Therefore, "sons of God" referred to in Genesis 6 should be interpreted as righteous men who had received God, in contrast with unrighteous men (*i.e.*, sons of men).

(2) Job 1: The sons of God Presented Themselves before God

Job describes an instance where "the sons of God came to present themselves before the Lord":

> Job 1:6 Now there was a day when *the sons of God came to present themselves before the Lord*, and Satan also came among them.

> Job 1:7 And the Lord said to Satan, "From where do you come?" So Satan answered the Lord and said, "From going to and fro on the earth, and from walking back and forth on it."

Here, the context makes clear that it refers not to men, but rather, to angels, since the "sons" had presented themselves before God, presumably within the heavenly realm.

(3) Job 38: The sons of God Shouted for Joy

Similarly, it can be presumed from context that by "sons of God," Job 38 refers to angels:

> Job 38:7 When the morning stars sang together, And all the sons of God shouted for joy?

(4) Psalms 82: You Are Gods and Children of the Most High

Psalms 82 states that we are all 'gods":

Psa 82:1 A Psalm of Asaph. God stands in the congregation of the mighty; He judges among the gods.

Psa 82:2 How long will you judge unjustly, And show partiality to the wicked? Selah

Psa 82:3 Defend the poor and fatherless; Do justice to the afflicted and needy.

Psa 82:4 Deliver the poor and needy; Free them from the hand of the wicked.

Psa 82:5 They do not know, nor do they understand; They walk about in darkness; All the foundations of the earth are unstable.

Psa 82:6 I said, "You are gods, And all of you are children of the Most High.

Psa 82:7 But you shall die like men, And fall like one of the princes."

Psa 82:8 Arise, O God, judge the earth; For You shall inherit all nations.

By "gods," the Psalmist is referring not to "gods" as divine beings, but rather, as rulers who, despite their power and authority, are ultimately mortals who "shall die like men, And fall like one of the princes" (Psa 82:6-7). "God" (capitalized) judges among the "gods" (lowercase), or rulers (Psa 82:1). Unlike God, the "gods," or rulers, judge unjustly and show partiality to the wicked (Psa 82:2). They "do not know, nor do they understand; They walk about in darkness; All the foundations of the earth are unstable" (Psa 82:5). This contrasts God, who "is righteous in all the works which He does, though we have not obeyed His voice" (Dan 9:14).

(5) Matthew 5: Peacemakers Shall Be Called Sons of God

Jesus states that the peacemakers are blessed, for they shall be called sons of God:

Mat 5:9 Blessed are the peacemakers, For they shall be called sons of God.

Mat 5:10 Blessed are those who are persecuted for righteousness' sake, For theirs is the kingdom of heaven.

Mat 5:11 "Blessed are you when they revile and persecute you, and say all kinds of evil against you falsely for My sake.

Here, Jesus is again referring to "sons of God" as those who receive God. They are peacemakers, and their fruit is the fruit of God. This is consistent with the way that "sons of God" is used in other areas of the Bible.

(6) Luke 20: The sons of God Who Attain Resurrection Neither Marry Nor are Given in Marriage

Luke writes:

Luke 20:34 Jesus answered and said to them, "The sons of this age marry and are given in marriage.

Luke 20:35 But those who are counted worthy to attain that age, and the resurrection from the dead, neither marry nor are given in marriage;

Luke 20:36 nor can they die anymore, for they are equal to the angels and are sons of God, being sons of the resurrection.

Luke 20:37 But even Moses showed in the burning bush passage that the dead are raised, when he called the Lord 'THE GOD OF ABRAHAM, THE GOD OF ISAAC, AND THE GOD OF JACOB.'

Jesus is again referring to those who have received God, but here, he speaks of them *after* they have attained resurrection from the dead; they are "counted worthy to attain that age and the resurrection from the dead" (Luke 20:37). Upon their resurrection, they "neither marry nor are given in marriage" (Luke 20:35). They become sons of God because they have received God and, after the resurrection, they are like angels in that they do not marry and cannot die.

The sons of God are contrasted from the sons of this age. The sons of this age marry and are given in marriage, but the sons of God:
- are counted worthy to attain that age and the resurrection from the dead (Luke 20:35);
- neither marry nor are given in marriage (Luke 20:35);
- cannot die anymore (Luke 20:36);
- are equal to the angels (Luke 20:36);
- are sons of the resurrection (Luke 20:36);

(7) Romans 8: The sons of God Are Led by the Spirit of God

Romans 8 states:

> Rom 8:12 Therefore, brethren, we are debtors--not to the flesh, to live according to the flesh.

> Rom 8:13 For if you live according to the flesh you will die; but if by the Spirit you put to death the deeds of the body, you will live.

> Rom 8:14 For as many as are led by the Spirit of God, these are sons of God.

> Rom 8:15 For you did not receive the spirit of bondage again to fear, but you received the Spirit of adoption by whom we cry out, "Abba, Father."

> Rom 8:16 The Spirit Himself bears witness with our spirit that we are children of God.

> Rom 8:17 and if children, then heirs--heirs of God and joint heirs with Christ, if indeed we suffer with Him, that we may also be glorified together.

> Rom 8:18 For I consider that the sufferings of this present time are not worthy to be compared with the glory which shall be revealed in us.

> Rom 8:19 For the earnest expectation of the creation eagerly waits for the revealing of the sons of God.

Here, Paul writes that if we live by the flesh, we will die, but if we live according to the Spirit, putting to death the deeds of the body, we will live (Rom 8:13). The sons of God are those who are "led by the Spirit of God" (Rom 8:14). We received the Spirit of adoption by whom we call God "Father" (Rom 8:15). When we receive the Spirit of God, we become children of God (Rom 8:16).

(8) Galatians 3: sons of God through Faith in Christ

Galatians states that we are sons of God through faith in Jesus Christ:

> Gal 3:22 But the Scripture has confined all under sin, that the promise by faith in Jesus Christ might be given to those who believe.

> Gal 3:23 But before faith came, we were kept under guard by the law, kept for the faith which would afterward be revealed.

Gal 3:24 Therefore the law was our tutor to bring us to Christ, that we might be justified by faith.

Gal 3:25 But after faith has come, we are no longer under a tutor.

Gal 3:26 For you are all sons of God through faith in Christ Jesus.

Gal 3:27 For as many of you as were baptized into Christ have put on Christ.

Gal 3:28 There is neither Jew nor Greek, there is neither slave nor free, there is neither male nor female; for you are all one in Christ Jesus.

Gal 3:29 And if you are Christ's, then you are Abraham's seed, and heirs according to the promise.

Here, we read that all are confined by sin under the law of the Scripture (Gal 3:22-24), but after faith came, we are no longer under the law Gal 3:25). We are now *sons of God through faith in Jesus Christ* (Gal 3:26).

c)

5. Conclusion

"Son of God" (in the singular), as used in the Old and New Testaments, can refer to any of the following:

- Jesus
  - o Jesus is referred to as the "Son of God" by Daniel (implied), the Centurion, the angel Gabriel, Jesus Himself (before the Sanhedrin, to Nicodemus, to the blind man, etc.), the apostles and disciples, Satan and the demons;
- Adam
  - o In Luke's genealogy, Adam was referred to as the "Son of God" in the sense that he was created by God (*i.e.*, he had no natural father), unlike in the *divine* sense in which Jesus is the Son of God (*i.e.*, as a member of the Trinity, begotten of the Father).
- In a figurative sense, as used with:

o   Israel (Jacob) to refer to God's people, the nation of Israel, rather than to any individual literal son;

o   David, who was "begotten" by God (Psa 2:7) and was God's "firstborn" (Psa 89:27). This, too, is meant figuratively, as David was the natural son of Jesse, not of God;

o   Solomon, who was referred to as God's son in a figurative sense, whereas Solomon was David's son in a literal sense.

"Sons of God" (in the plural), as used in the Old and New Testaments, can have two meanings:

-   Righteous Men

o   Genesis 6 refers to the sons of God as righteous men who took unrighteous women (the daughters of man) as their wives;

o   Matthew 5 refers to sons of God as peacemakers;

o   Luke 20 refers to the sons of God who attain resurrection and neither marry nor are given in marriage, but are like the angels;

o   Romans 8 refers to sons of God as led by the Spirit of God;

o   Galatians 3 refers to those who are sons of God through Faith in Christ.

-   Angels

o   Job 1 refers to the sons of God, who are angels that presented themselves before God;

o   Job 38 refers to angles as sons of God shouting for joy.

On the basis of the foregoing, we can conclude that the terms "son of God" or "sons of God" have a meaning distinct from that given to Jesus as the "only begotten Son of God." "Sons" and "son" of God can refer to:

-   Adam;

-   Israel (the nation), David and Solomon, who are spiritual sons of God;

-   righteous men, who are the physical offspring of natural men but are the spiritual sons of God and joint heirs with Christ through faith in Christ;

-   the angels, who are created directly by God.

In contrast, the "Son of God" refers to Jesus.

E. John 1:1 States that the Word was "a God," not "God"

1. Argument

Dr. Philips argues as follows (p. 55):

> The Greek word for 'God' used in the phrase "and the Word was with God," is the definite form *hotheos*, meaning 'The God'. However, in the second phrase "and the Word was God', the Greek word used for 'God' is the indefinite form *tontheos*, which means 'a god'. Consequently, John 1:1, should more accurately be translated, "In the beginning was the Word, and the Word was with God, and the Word was a god."

John 1:1 states as follows in the NKJV:

> John 1:1 In the beginning was the Word, and the Word was with God, and the Word was God.

The original Greek of John 1:1 states as follows:

> Και θεος ην ο λογος
>
> *Kahee theh'-os i-mee' ho log'-os*

With Strong's numbers, it states:

> καιG2532 CONJ θεοςG2316 N-NSM ηνG1510 V-IAI-3S oG3588 T-NSM λογοςG3056 N-NSM

This literally translates as:

> a god was the Word (i.e., the Word "was a god," rather than "was God")

2. Explanation 1: The Context of John 1:1 Makes Clear that the Translation Should Be "God" Rather than "a God"

a) Overview

CARM.org advocates for a contextual reading of John 1:1, arguing that a translation of John 1:1 that the Word was "a God" rather than "God" is the only one that makes sense in light of the context and the fact that John, a devout Jew, could not have argued for a polytheistic characterization of the Word in relation to God.

Specifically, CARM.org argues that the Jehovah's Witnesses' New World Translation, which translates the verse as stating that the Word was "a god," is incorrect due to the following[30]:

> First of all, the Bible teaches a strict monotheism. To say that Jesus is "a god" is to suggest that there is another god besides YHWH, which is contrary to scripture (Isaiah 43:10; 44:6, 8, etc.).
>
> John was a strict Jew, a monotheist. Does the Jehovah's Witness really think that John would be saying that there was another God besides Jehovah even if it were Jesus? Being raised a good Jew, the Apostle John would never believe that there was more than one God in existence. Yet, he compared the word with God, said the word was God, and that the word became flesh (John 1:1, 14).
>
> …
>
> Is there suddenly a new god in the text of John 1:1? It is the same God that is being spoken of in part 2 as in part 3. How do the Jehovah's Witnesses maintain that the word had somehow become a god in this context since there is only one God mentioned? Remember, the Jehovah's Witnesses teach that Jesus was Michael the Archangel. Therefore, is there any place in the Bible where an angel is called "a god" besides Satan being called the god of this world in 2 Cor. 4:3-4?
>
> John 20:28--"Thomas answered and said to Him, 'My Lord and my God!'"
>
> In the Greek in John 20:28 Thomas said to Jesus, "ho kurios mou, kai ho theos mou," "The Lord of me, and the God of me." If Jesus was not God, but "a" god, then shouldn't Jesus have corrected Thomas? Shouldn't Jesus have said, "No, Thomas, I am not the God. I am a god."? But Jesus did not. To do so would have been ludicrous. Nevertheless, the Jehovah's Witness will say that Thomas was so stunned by Jesus' appearance that he swore. This is ridiculous because it means that Thomas, a devout man of God, swore in front of Jesus and used the Lord's name in vain in violation of Exodus 20:7. This is hardly the case since we find no New Testament equivalent of a disciple of Christ using God's name in vain.

---

[30] See <https://carm.org/john-1-1-word-was-god>.

In conclusion, John 1:1 is best translated without the "a" inserted into the text. "The Word was God" is the best translation. This way, we do not run into the danger of polytheism with Jesus being "a god." We do not have Thomas the disciple swearing and using God's name in vain; and, we do not have the problem of Jesus being a "mighty god" and yet not the God--even though God Himself is called the Mighty God (Jeremiah 32:18; Isaiah 10:21).

b) *Response*

The central problem with CARM.org's contextual explanation is that it first concludes that there is one God and, on this basis, argues that any translation that states otherwise cannot be a valid translation. In other words, it aligns what it deems to be a valid translation with the conclusion that it purports to represent true Christianity. Therefore, if a manuscript had been produced that stated in the original Greek that there were "two gods," CARM.org's response would be to state that the translation "two gods" is inaccurate, regardless of the fact that the actual Greek stated the same.

This approach to resolving contradictions in the Bible is circular. If Muslims were permitted to adopt this approach to addressing apparent contradictions in the Qur'ān, they would always be able to explain contradictions by arguing for a translation of the original Arabic that removes the contradiction. They could then argue that because the Qur'ān cannot contradict itself, any translation of the Qur'ān that contains a contradiction cannot be valid. Of course, such an approach would not resolve the problem with the contradiction in the original Arabic text any more than CARM.org's approach resolves the problem with the original Greek text, which states:

Και θεος ην ο λογος

καιG2532 CONJ θεοςG2316 N-NSM ηνG1510 V-IAI-3S oG3588 T-NSM λογοςG3056 N-NSM

This literally translates as:

a god was the Word (i.e., the Word "was a god," rather than "was God")

CARM.org repeats this approach by arguing that any translation of John 1:1 that suggests polytheism is invalid, even if such a translation is an accurate rendering of the original Greek. CARM.org states[31]:

> Furthermore, how many actual gods are there in scripture? The obvious answer is that there is only one God in existence. Though there are others who have been falsely called gods (1 Cor. 8:5-6) or even said to be "as God" like Moses (Ex. 4:16; 7:1), there is only one real God (Gal. 4:8-9; Isaiah 44:6, 8). If Jesus is "a god" that was "with God" in the beginning, then is Jesus a true god or a false god?

3.   Explanation 2: The Original Greek Text of John 1:1 Refers to "God," Not "a God"

a)   Overview

CARM.org does give some attention to the original text of John 1:1 by employing a textual argument. This textual argument is stronger than the contextual argument noted above. Specifically, CARM.org argues as follows[32]:

> John 1:1 in a literal translation reads thus: "In beginning was the word, and the word was with the God, and God was the word." Notice that it says "God was the word." This is the actual word-for-word translation. It is not saying that "a god was the word." That wouldn't make sense. Let me break it down into three statements.
>
> "In beginning was the word . . . "
> (en   arche   en ho logos)
> A very simple statement that the Word was in the beginning.
>
> "and the word was with the God . . . "
> (kai ho logos en pros ton theon)
> This same Word was with God.
>
> "and God was the word."--Properly translated as "and the Word was God."
> (kai theos en ho logos)
> This same Word was God.

[31] See <https://carm.org/john-1-1-word-was-god>.
[32] See <https://carm.org/john-1-1-word-was-god>.

Regarding statement 3 above, the correct English translation is ". . . and the Word was God" and not "and God was the word." This is because if there is only one definite article ("ho"="the") in a clause where two nouns are in the nominative ("subject") form ("theos" and "logos"), then the noun with the definite article ("ho"="the") is the subject. In this case "ho logos" means that "the word" is the subject of the clause. Therefore, " . . . the Word was God" is the correct translation and not "God was the Word."1 But this does not negate the idea that John is speaking of only one God, not two, even though the Jehovah's Witnesses maintain that Jesus is "a god" or the "mighty god" as was addressed above.

b) Response

CARM.org is inaccurate in rendering the Greek "kai theos en ho logos" as "This same Word was God." A more accurate literal rendition is:

Και	θεος	ην	ο	λογος
and	a god	was	the	Word

or:

	and	God	was	the	Word

The Greek θεος can be translated as either "a god" or as "God" because there is no definite article before "God." CARM.org does not adequately address this issue. This bridges us to the next explanation, which is perhaps the most satisfying one.

4. Explanation 3: The Greek θεος Generally Means "God," Not "a God"

The Christian Courier advances an explanation that is the most satisfying. In essence, it argues that the Greek θεος can be translated as either "a god" or as "God" because there is no definite article before "God," but the translation "God" is more apt given the definite article before θεον in the first part of the verse. Also, the Christian Courier shows that if the absence of the article in θεον meant that the term had to be translated as "a god," then even the Jehovah's witnesses, who

advance the "a god" translation in John 1:1, would be in violation of
their own rule. The Christian Courier has written[33]:

> The noun theos is found some 1,343 times in the Greek Testament
> (Smith, 173). According to one scholar who has researched the
> matter considerably, in no fewer than 282 of these texts theos is
> without the article (Countess, 54-55).

> If the Watchtower contrived translation rule is valid, we would
> expect to find the rendition "a god" in each of these passages.

> But that isn't the case. In only sixteen instances of The New World
> Translation (6% of the total) do we find the rendition as "a god,"
> "god," "gods" or "godly."

> Even in the context of John 1:1-18, where theos is found without the
> article on six occasions (cf., 1:1, 2, 6, 12, 13, 18), it is only rendered
> as "a god" or "god" twice (vv. 1, 18) in the New World Translation.
> Even the Witnesses do not follow their own, self-imposed rule.

F. *The Myth of God Incarnate,* by John Hick

1. Overview

Dr. Philips writes (p. 59-60):

> Today, there are many modern scholars in Christianity who hold
> that Jesus Christ was not God. In 1977, a group of seven biblical
> scholars, including leading Anglican theologians and other New
> Testament scholars, published a book called *The Myth of God
> Incarnate*, which caused a great uproar in the General Synod of the
> Church of England. In the preface, the editor, John Hick, wrote the
> following: "The writers of this book are convinced that another
> major theological development is called for in this last part of the
> twentieth century. The need arises from growing knowledge of
> Christian origins, and involves a recognition that Jesus was (as he is
> presented in Acts 2.21) 'a man approved by God' for a special role
> within the divine purpose, and that *the later conception of him as
> God incarnate, the Second Person of the Holy Trinity living a*

---

[33] See <https://www.christiancourier.com/articles/774-what-about-that-a-god-translation-in-the-jehovahs-witness-bible>.

human life, is a mythological or poetic way of expressing his significance for us."

There is a *broad agreement among New Testament scholars that the historical Jesus did not make the claim to deity that later Christian thought was to make for him; he did not understand himself to be God*, or God the Son, incarnate [in the flesh].108 The late Archbishop Michael Ramsey, who was himself a New Testament scholar, wrote that "Jesus did not claim deity for himself." His contemporary, the New Testament scholar C.F.D. Moule, said that, "Any case for a 'high' Christology that depended on the authenticity of the alleged claims of Jesus about himself, especially in the Fourth Gospel, would indeed be precarious."

2. Response

a) Overview

In response to *The Myth of God Incarnate*, it is only necessary to point out the overwhelming scriptural references in support of Jesus' divinity. When confronted by these references, the skeptic must either concede that Jesus claimed to be God or argue that the Scriptures do not reliably recount His words. It is not, however, possible to maintain that in the Gospels, Jesus denied being God or that he did not claim to be God. His acceptance of worship and names fitting for God alone are beyond doubt.

b) Jesus Did Not Deny Being the Son of God

In reality, Jesus never actually rejected the title Son of God. Rebuking the demons is not the equivalent of denying His divinity. In Mark 5, there is an instance where a demon identified Jesus as the Son of God, and Jesus again did not deny the title:

> Mark 5:7 And he cried out with a loud voice and said, "What have I to do with You, Jesus, Son of the Most High God? I implore You by God that You do not torment me."
>
> Mark 5:8 For He said to him, "Come out of the man, unclean spirit!"
>
> Mark 5:9 Then He asked him, "What is your name?" And he answered, saying, "My name is Legion; for we are many."

c)   *Verses that Explicitly State that Jesus is the Son of God*
Many other verses establish His divinity. For example:

(1) Jesus Proclaimed to be God before the Sandrehin (Mat 26)
Jesus proclaimed to be God before the Sandrehin:

> Mat 26:63 But Jesus kept silent. And the high priest answered and
> said to Him, "I put You under oath by the living God: Tell us if You
> are the Christ, the Son of God!"

> Mat 26:64 Jesus said to him, "It is as you said. Nevertheless, I say to
> you, hereafter you will see the Son of Man sitting at the right hand
> of the Power, and coming on the clouds of heaven."

> Mat 26:65 Then the high priest tore his clothes, saying, "He has
> spoken blasphemy! What further need do we have of witnesses?
> Look, now you have heard His blasphemy!

(2) Jesus Acknowledged before Pontius Pilate that He was King of a
Heavenly Kingdom (John 18)
Jesus acknowledged before Pontius Pilate that He was the king of the
Jews, but that His kingdom was not of this world. He therefore implied
that He was a divine king, which is consistent with His claim of being
the Son of God:

> John 18:36 Jesus answered, "My kingdom is not of this world. If My
> kingdom were of this world, My servants would fight, so that I
> should not be delivered to the Jews; but now My kingdom is not
> from here."

> John 18:37 Pilate therefore said to Him, "Are You a king then?"
> Jesus answered, "You say rightly that I am a king. For this cause I
> was born, and for this cause I have come into the world, that I
> should bear witness to the truth. Everyone who is of the truth hears
> My voice."

(3) Jesus Praised Peter for Calling Him the Son of God (Mat 16)
Rather than deny that He was the son of God or chastise Peter, Jesus
praised Peter when Peter confessed that Jesus was "the Christ, the Son of
the living God" (Mat 16:16):

> Mat 16:15 He said to them, "But who do you say that I am?"

Mat 16:16 Simon Peter answered and said, "You are the Christ, the Son of the living God."

Mat 16:17 Jesus answered and said to him, "Blessed are you, Simon Bar-Jonah, for flesh and blood has not revealed this to you, but My Father who is in heaven.

G. The New Testament Allegedly Claims that Jesus was Only a Prophet

1. Argument

Next, Dr. Philips argues that according to the New Testament, Jesus claimed to be only a prophet. Dr. Philips cites a host of verses to support this argument, including, for example, Mat 21:11:

So the multitudes said, "This is Jesus, the prophet from Nazareth of Galilee."

Dr. Philips also quotes John 17:3:

And this is eternal life, that they may know You, the only true God, and Jesus Christ whom You have sent.

2. Response

Of course, the New Testament maintains that Jesus was a prophet. But it does not deny that he was more than a prophet. Indeed, Jesus claimed to be more than a messenger; he was indeed the son of God and one with God. There is made crystal clear when Jesus confirms to the High Priest that He is the Son of God.

Mat 26:63 But Jesus kept silent. And the high priest answered and said to Him, "I put You under oath by the living God: Tell us if You are the Christ, the Son of God!"

Mat 26:64 Jesus said to him, "It is as you said. Nevertheless, I say to you, hereafter you will see the Son of Man sitting at the right hand of the Power, and coming on the clouds of heaven."

In Matthew 16, Jesus asks the disciples who they believe He is. When Peter replied stating that Jesus was the Son of God, Jesus praised him and said that Peter was the rock on which Jesus would build his church (Mat 16:13-18):

> Mat 16:13 When Jesus came into the region of Caesarea Philippi, He asked His disciples, saying, "Who do men say that I, the Son of Man, am?"

> Mat 16:14 So they said, "Some say John the Baptist, some Elijah, and others Jeremiah or one of the prophets."

> Mat 16:15 He said to them, "But who do you say that I am?"

> Mat 16:16 Simon Peter answered and said, "You are the Christ, the Son of the living God."

> Mat 16:17 Jesus answered and said to him, "Blessed are you, Simon Bar-Jonah, for flesh and blood has not revealed this to you, but My Father who is in heaven.

> Mat 16:18 And I also say to you that you are Peter, and on this rock I will build My church, and the gates of Hades shall not prevail against it.

In reply to this argument, Islam argues that the verses in question are corruptions that were later added to the Scriptures. Of course, there is no way to respond to the circular argument that those verses that conform to Islamic doctrine are faithful to the original revelation, whereas those that contradict Islamic doctrine are later additions and corruptions.

H. Survey Reveals More than Half of England's Anglican Bishops Say Christians Are Not Obliged to Believe Jesus was God

1. Overview

Dr. Philips next quotes a story that supposedly appeared in the Daily News on 25 June 1984 under the heading "Shock survey of Anglican bishops." The news story is alleged to have stated:

> More than half of England's Anglican Bishops say that Christians are not obliged to believe that Jesus Christ was God, according to a survey published today. The pole of 31 of England's 39 bishops shows that many of them think that Christ's miracles, the virgin birth and the resurrection might not have happened exactly as described in the Bible. Only 11 of the bishops insisted that Christians must regard Christ as both God and man, while 19 said it was sufficient to regard Jesus as 'God's supreme agent.'

This article is offered by Dr. Philips as evidence of "the degree to which there are doubts among the clergy regarding Jesus' divinity."

2. Response

Dr. Philips' argument is flawed on multiple levels:

a) *Evidence of Doubt of Jesus' Divinity is Not Evidence against His Divinity*

The relevance of the article in question is not immediately clear. Even if it can be shown that more than half of England's bishops denied that Jesus was God, this is in no way evidence that He is, in fact, not God. There is no shortage of heretics, apostates and heretical groups and teachings, including the following:

- In ancient times:
  - o Nazarenes
  - o Ebionites
  - o Arians
  - o Nestorians
  - o Monophysites
  - o Monothelitites
- In modern times:
  - o Church of Jesus Christ of Latter Day Saints (Mormons)[34]
  - o Jehovah's Witnesses
  - o Church of Christ, Scientist[35]
  - o Scientology[36]

---

[34] The Church of Jesus Christ of Latter Day Saints follow the *Book of Mormon* and the Bible.

[35] Led by Mary Eddy Baker, the Church of Christ, Scientist holds that sickness is an illusion that can be corrected by prayer alone. Mary Eddy Baker's book, *Science and Health*, became Christian Science's central text, along with the Bible, and by 2001 had sold over nine million copies. Its adherents believe that reality is purely spiritual, the material world an illusion, disease is a mental error rather than physical disorder and the sick should be treated not by medicine but by a form of prayer that seeks to correct the beliefs responsible for the illusion of ill health.

[36] Founded by L. Ron Hubbard, human Scientology holds that a human is an immortal, spiritual being (thetan) that is resident in a physical body. The thetan has had innumerable past lives. Moreover, lives preceding the thetan's arrival on Earth were lived in extraterrestrial cultures.

    o   International Church of Christ (considered by some to be a cult or to have cult-like characteristics[37])

The fact that there are so many heretical groups does not in any way detract from orthodox Christianity. In fact, even the denial of a majority of self-professed Christians would not detract from the truth of Scripture. Christ said "narrow is the gate and difficult is the way which leads to life" (Mat 7:14), meaning that most people would take the easy path, which his the path of destruction. Heresy has been around since the earliest days of Christianity, with groups such as the Nazarenes and Ebionites denying Jesus' divinity. Yet Christianity does not base its authority on its popularity or the fact that it is free from heresy. If that were the criterion for judging the truth of religion, then Islam too would have problems, given a great number of prominent scholars who deny basic truths deemed to be core to the Muslim faith.[38]

b) *The Supposed Article Does Not Appear to Ever Have Been Published, Nor Does There Appear to Have Been a London-Based Newspaper Called "Daily News"*

The supposed article "Shock Survey of Anglican Bishops" does not appear to ever have existed or been published. A search for the article through online search engines turns out only Islamic proselytic websites and books exploiting the article as evidence that Jesus was not God. Such web sites include:

- http://www.answering-christianity.com/ac/ang.htm; and
- https://truereligiondebate.wordpress.com.

Such books include:

---

[37] Others consider the International Church of Christ to hold orthodox doctrines but to exercise excessive control over its members.

[38] For example, Reza Aslan, a Muslim scholar, believes that Jesus was crucified and questions Jesus' virgin birth. Admitting the crucifixion and denying the virgin birth both contradict core doctrines of the Qur'ān. *See* "Interview on 'Zealot: The Life and Times of Jesus of Nazareth,'" available at <https://genius.com/Reza-aslan-interview-on-zealot-the-life-and-times-of-jesus-of-nazareth-annotated> (in response to the question, "How are your findings different from what Islam actually believes about Jesus?," Aslan states that "Islam doesn't believe that Jesus was crucified, first of all. Islam believes in the virgin birth. I mean-- Jesus was most definitely crucified, and my book does question the historicity of the virgin birth").
, flatly denying Qur'anic verses that state that He was substituted on the cross.

- Dil R Banu's *One God for All*; and
- Islam Kotob's *Trinity Doctrine Divinely Inspired*.

What is particularly notable in the latter work, *Trinity Doctrine Divinely Inspired*, is that it does not cite to the alleged *Daily News* article itself, but rather, to other Islamic proselytic sources that cite the source. The following citation is used (p. 46):

> Shock Survey of Anglican Bishops: *Daily News, U.K.*, 25 / 6 / 84, (source: Islamic Propagation Centre International, 20 Green Lane, Small Heath, Birmingham B9 5DB, Tel. 021-773- 0137).

The authenticity of the alleged article is so dubious that Islamic proselytic materials must cite to other Islamic proselytic materials as the source of the alleged article rather than to the article itself, or to a link to the *Daily News* where the article is published or to an archive that has preserved the supposed article. This raises the question as to whether the article ever did exist, or whether it is merely an invention of Islamic proselytes ever eager to impugn the divinity of Jesus Christ.

In fact, the very publication in which the alleged article is supposed to have been published in, *Daily News*, does not even appear to exist as a newspaper. An online search for "*Daily News*" does not uncover any such publication. The alleged article was supposedly published in London, but a search for "London *Daily News*" does not turn up any relevant results either. This casts the arguments of these proselytes into even further doubt and suggests that the article is either some kind of a hoax or an invention of Islamic proselytes to further their cause.

c) The Mathematical Reasoning in the Article is Flawed

The article is mathematically flawed. It allegedly states as follows:

> More than half of England's Anglican Bishops say that Christians are not obliged to believe that Jesus Christ was God, according to a survey published today. The pole of 31 of England's 39 bishops shows that many of them think that Christ's miracles, the virgin birth and the resurrection might not have happened exactly as described in the Bible. Only 11 of the bishops insisted that Christians must regard Christ as both God and man, while 19 said it was sufficient to regard Jesus as 'God's supreme agent.' One declined to give a definite opinion.

If the article is real, it makes the following allegations:

- More than half of England's Anglican Bishops say that Christians are not obliged to believe that Jesus Christ was God.
- 31 of England's 39 bishops were polled.
- Only 11 of the bishops that were polled (i.e., 11 out of 31) insisted that Christians must regard Christ as both God and man.
- Therefore, 20 out of the 31 polled did not insist that Christians must regard Christ as both God and man.
  - o Of these 20 that did not insist that Christians must regard Christ as both God and man, only 19 said it was sufficient to regard Jesus as "God's supreme agent."
  - o The position of the 20th bishop is unknown, for he "declined to give a definite opinion."

We thus only know the positions of 30 of the bishops, as follows:

- 11 insisted that Christians must regard Christ as both God and man;
- 19 said it was sufficient to regard Jesus as "God's supreme agent."
- We do not know the position of the remaining 9 bishops:
  - o 1 of the bishops declined to give an opinion, so it is possible that he sides with the 11 bishops that insisted that Christians must regard Christ as both God and man;
  - o 8 of the bishops were never polled. It is possible that all of them insisted that Christians must regard Christ as both God and man.
- If all 9 of the bishops whose opinions remain unknown side with the 11 bishops who insist that Christians must regard Christ as both God and man, then a total of 20 of the Anglican bishops would insist that Christians must regard Christ as both God and man. This would be a majority of the total of England's 39 bishops.

Therefore, by stating that "More than half of England's Anglican Bishops say that Christians are not obliged to believe that Jesus Christ was God," the article assumes that at least one of the 9 bishops whose opinions remain unknown believe it is sufficient to regard Jesus as "God's supreme agent." However, this is a faulty assumption as no evidence is proferred to suggest what any of the 8 bishops believe, one way or another. Therefore, the conclusion of the article is flawed. The flaw in the article's reasoning further casts into doubt the reliability of the entire article, since the author likely practiced the same degree of negligence in gathering his or her facts as he or she did in drawing the conclusions.

d) The Statement of the Article Contradicts the Plain Statement of Faith Published by the Anglican Church

The statement of faith published by the Anglican Church's "What we believe" webpage states very clearly that Jesus is God's Son and God[39]:

> Belief in God as *Father*, *Son* and *Holy Spirit* is at the heart of our faith.

In other words, the Jesus Christ is "God," not "God's supreme agent," as the survey suggests.

The "What we believe" webpage also makes clear that Jesus is God's Son.

> Christians believe that Jesus is God's Son … God has revealed himself most clearly through the gift of his Son, Jesus Christ.

The "What we believe" webpage also cites to the Apostles' Creed, which also affirms Jesus' divinity and sonship. It states that Jesus is both God's "Son" and our "Lord":

> I believe in God, the Father almighty, creator of heaven and earth.
>
> I believe in *Jesus Christ, his only Son, our Lord*, who was conceived by the Holy Spirit, born of the Virgin Mary, suffered under Pontius Pilate, was crucified, died, and was buried; he descended to the dead. On the third day he rose again; he ascended into heaven, he is seated at the right hand of the Father, and he will come to judge the living and the dead.
>
> I believe in the Holy Spirit, the holy Catholic Church, the communion of saints, the forgiveness of sins, the resurrection of the body, and the life everlasting. Amen.

---

[39] Available at <https://www.churchofengland.org/our-faith/what-we-believe>.

Chapter 6. Arguments in Favor of Islam

A. Allegation that the *Qur'ān* Is Uncorrupt

1. General Argument

a) Overview

Next, Dr. Philips goes on to argue that unlike the Bible, which has been corrupted over the ages, Prophet Muhammad's message has been divinely preserved over the centuries. Dr. Philips quotes the orientalist John Burton, who stated that the text of the *Qur'ān* available today is "the text which has come down to us in the form in which it was organized and approved by the Prophet... What we have today in our hands is the muṣḥaf of Muhammad" (p. 30).

b) Response

Dr. Philips quotes John Burton, but there are many others who can be quoted who allege that the Quranic text has been corrupted. The article "Is the Quran Preserved?," for example, states "how can we trust that the Quran is preserved if these three Revelations are corrupted?"[40]

Dr. Philips himself concedes (p. 30-31):

> the "Institute fur Koranforschung" of the University of Munich, Germany, collected and collated over 42,000 complete or incomplete copies of the Qur'aan. After some fifty years of study, they reported that in terms of differences between the various copies, there were no variants, except occasional mistakes of copyists, which could easily be ascertained.

---

[40] Available at <https://www.answering-islam.org/Authors/Khaled/quran_preserved.htm>.

Dr. Philips concedes that there have been occasional mistakes of copyists of the *Qur'ān*. The discrepancies found in modern translations of the Bible can be attributed to these same copyist errors, to wit:

- Jehoiachin's age when he became king, to which the NIV Study Bible states there are discrepancies between one Hebrew manuscript, some Septuagint manuscripts, and Syriac on the one hand, and most Hebrew manuscripts on the other;

- Whether Amminadab was the son of Ram, Arni, or Admin in Luke 3:33 varies in some manuscripts.

There is no evidence that such errors can be attributed to deliberate manipulation of the Bible by the Church; there could be no incentive to change innocuous facts such as Jehoiachin's age or the name of Amminadab's father, which have no bearing on Christian doctrine or the central teachings of Jesus and the prophets. Clearly, then, the *Qur'ān* has been subject to the same inevitable issue of copyist error whenever an ancient text is transmitted over hundreds of years to later generations.

2. Explanation of Apparent Contradiction between *'Āyah* 6:14 and *'Āyah* 7:143

a) Overview

Next, Dr. Philips seeks to address the apparent contradiction between *'Āyah* 6:14, where Muhammad states that he is the first "of those who submit," and 7:143, which states that Moses is "the first of the believers":

> 6:14. Say: Shall I take for a friend other than Allah, the Originator of the heavens and the earth, and He feeds and is not fed? Say: I am commanded to be the first of those who submit. And be thou not of the polytheists.

قُلْ أَغَيْرَ اللَّهِ أَتَّخِذُ وَلِيًّا فَاطِرِ السَّمَاوَاتِ وَالْأَرْضِ وَهُوَ يُطْعِمُ وَلَا يُطْعَمُ قُلْ إِنِّي أُمِرْتُ أَنْ أَكُونَ أَوَّلَ مَنْ أَسْلَمَ وَلَا تَكُونَنَّ مِنَ الْمُشْرِكِينَ.

> 7:143. So when his Lord manifested His glory to the mountain, He made it crumble and Moses fell down in a swoon. Then when he recovered, he said: Glory be to Thee! I turn to Thee, and I am the first of the believers.

فَلَمَّا تَجَلَّى رَبُّهُ لِلْجَبَلِ جَعَلَهُ دَكًّا وَخَرَّ مُوسَى صَعِقًا فَلَمَّا أَفَاقَ قَالَ سُبْحَانَكَ تُبْتُ إِلَيْكَ وَأَنَا أَوَّلُ الْمُؤْمِنِينَ.

Dr. Philips responds to this apparent contradiction as follows (p. 32):

> The earlier verse refers to Prophet Muhammad, who was told to inform the pagans of his time that he could never accept their idolatry and would be the first of those in his time to submit to Allaah. In the second verse, Prophet Moses declares himself among the first in his time to submit to Allaah upon realizing that it was impossible to see Allaah. Each prophet was the first in his own era to submit to Allaah.

b) Response

(1) Muhammad the First to Submit

That Muhammad would state that he is commanded to be the first of those who submit (i.e., the first "Muslim") is inconsistent with the Islamic doctrine that Muhammad was only one of many Muslim prophets, beginning with Adam and continuing with Ibrāhīm (Abraham), Mūsá (Moses), Eliyās (Elisha), Ayyūb (Job), Da'ūd (David), 'Isá (Jesus), and many others. Islam holds that Allah called all of these prophets to be Muslims to submit to His (*i.e.*, Allah's) will.

Dr. Philips attempts to get around this problem by stating that Muhammad was told to be "the first of those *in his time* to submit to Allaah" (p. 32). However, the Qur'ān does not include the clause "in his time." Rather, it simply states that Muhammad would be the "first of those who submit themselves" to Allah (أُمِرْتُ أَنْ أَكُونَ أَوَّلَ مَنْ أَسْلَمَ) (*'Āyah* 1:173). This is inconsistent with a fundamental Islamic doctrine.

(2) Moses the First of the Believers

As per the *Qur'ān*, Moses stated that he was "the first of the believers" (*'Āyah* 7:143). However, Islamic doctrine teaches that all of the prophets, beginning with Adam, believed in Allah. Dr. Philips attempts to circumvent this issue by arguing as follows (p. 32):

> Prophet Moses declares himself among the first *in his time* to submit to Allaah upon realizing that it was impossible to see Allaah. Each prophet was the first in his own era to submit to Allaah.

Once again, Dr. Philips attempts to explain the evident contradiction by inserting language that is not in the original text. In *'Āyah* 1:173, Moses simply states that he was the "first of the believers" (أَوَّلُ الْمُؤْمِنِينَ),

not the first of the believers "in his time." Dr. Philips' explanation is extra-textual and thus problematic.

B. Allegation that the Bible is Corrupt

1. Overview

Dr. Philips writes (p. 34):

> as stated in the Qur'aan, all scriptures revealed before the Qur'aan have not remained as they were revealed. People changed parts of them to suit their own desires.

Dr. Philips then quotes 'Āyah 2:79:

> Woe! then to those who write the Book with their hands then say, This is from God; so that they may take for it a small price. So woe! to them for what their hands write and woe! to them for what they earn.

Finally, he quotes Jeremiah 8:8:

> "How can you say, 'We are wise, And the law of the Lord is with us'? Look, the false pen of the scribe certainly works falsehood.

2. Response

a) Dr. Philips' Response is Inapposite

Dr. Philips confuses two separate issues. The first issue is that *Allāh* evidently issued his revelation to Moses, David, and Jesus, but then failed to preserve that revelation and allowed man to corrupt it. The second issue is that men have created false religions and teachings. The two are not necessarily the same. For example, Judaism and Christianity recognize that men can create false religions at the same time that the message given to Moses, Ezra, David, Solomon, Isaiah, Jeremiah, Ezekiel, Daniel, Hosea, Joel, Amos, Obadiah, Micah, Nahum, Habakkuk, Zephaniah, Haggai, Zechariah, Malachi, and Jesus were preserved. Therefore, the way to justify or prove that the Bible has been corrupted is not to show that there have been false teachers and messengers throughout history; Jews and Christians already acknowledge this. Rather, it is to show that the Biblical message is unreliable on the basis of historical or scientific evidence or that the Bible is self-contradictory.

b) The Corruption of the Bible Evidences Allāh's Weakness

Judaism and Christianity hold that while false teachings and false religions exist, God is not so impotent that he cannot preserve his Word from the distortions and corruptions of false prophets. This message is fundamentally at odds with Islam, which reconciles the contradictions between Islam and Christianity by holding that *Allāh* allowed for the Bible in its original form to become corrupted.

C. While the Bible Is Corrupt, Those Parts that Coincide with Islam Were Preserved and Are Free from Corruption

1. Overview

Next, Dr. Philips presents the argument that while the Bible Is corrupt, those parts that coincide with Christianity were preserved. He writes (p. 36):

> … the Biblical scriptures, both New and Old Testaments, are unreliable sources and cannot, therefore, be used as an authentic means of knowing the truth about the man called Jesus Christ or about his mission and message. However, a close examination of these scriptures in the light of Qur'aanic verses will reveal some of the truths about Jesus that have survived in the Bible.

2. Response

This is a clever but disingenuous argument. Essentially, it allows any false prophet to hijack a religion by arguing that his message is restoring the religion's message to its original and authentic truth by removing those doctrines that had been corrupted and preserving those that are true to the original text. The false prophet can claim proof for his new religion by preaching to would-be believers, "See! My message is corrupted by such-and-such verses from your text! Therefore, I am in the line of your prophets and am revealing the same message that your God revealed to the prophets," but when he is challenged by contradictions between his message and theirs, he will argue that the contradictions are due to corruptions to original religion. This clever tactic conveniently allows for no criticism of the new religion – those elements of the original religion that coincide with the new are offered as evidence that the new religion is a revelation by the same God, but those elements that contradict the new religion are offered as proof that the original religion was corrupted.

Chapter 7. Claims about the Corruption of the Bible

A. The Qur'ān Teaches that Jesus Confirmed the Torah; Therefore, Muslims Should Believe the Bible

1. Overview

Dr. Philips writes on p. 36 that Jesus, in *'Āyah* 61:6, confirmed the Torah. The *'Āyah* states:

> 61:6. And when Jesus, son of Mary, said O Children of Israel, surely I am the messenger of Allah to you, *verifying that which is before me of the Torah* …

وَإِذْ قَالَ عِيسَى ابْنُ مَرْيَمَ يَا بَنِي إِسْرَائِيلَ إِنِّي رَسُولُ اللهِ إِلَيْكُمْ *مُصَدِّقًا لِمَا بَيْنَ يَدَيَّ مِنَ التَّوْرَاةِ* ...

The original Arabic literally means "conforming that which is between my hands from the Torah" (مُصَدِّقًا لِمَا بَيْنَ يَدَيَّ مِنَ التَّوْرَاةِ). In other Words, Jesus had "in his hands" at the time of his teaching and preaching in the first century a copy of the Torah that he believed was trustworthy. If he believed the copy that he had was corrupted, he would not have said that he was confirming it. Rather, he would have stated something to the effect of, "I am confirming the original version of the Torah, not the corrupted version that I have in my hands."

This must mean that the Torah that Jesus quoted in the first century was authentic, and that it would have been corrupted thereafter. However, the Torah that we have today is identical to that of the first century, and even earlier texts. Therefore, the Torah that Jesus was quoting in the first century is identical to the Torah that we have today, and Jesus's affirmation of the Torah in *'Āyah* 61:6 corroborates that even Jesus, an esteemed prophet of God in Islam, confirmed the Torah. If Jesus believed in and confirmed the Torah of the First Century, then Muslims should do the same and should therefore reject Islamic teachings that contradict the Torah, including the teaching that Ishmael was the promised son of Abraham.

2. The Torah that Jesus Taught from Exists Today in the Dead Sea Scrolls

"Scholarly consensus dates [the Dead Sea Scrolls] from the last three centuries BCE and the first century CE."[41] If this is true, then it would appear that today, we have the Old Testament texts that were in circulation at the time of Jesus (i.e., the same texts that Jesus would have taught or read from, such as when he read Isaiah in the synagogue, as recounted in Luke 4:16-21). So if Islam is true, the corruption of the Torah would have had to occur after the life of Jesus.

3. Possible Islamic Response

Islam could respond that at the time of Jesus, two versions of the Torah had been circulating: one authentic and one corrupted. The one that Jesus had been speaking of in *'Āyah* 61:6 was the authentic Torah and, over the centuries, false teachers obliterated all copies of the authentic Torah, leaving only copies of the corrupted text in circulation.

B. Jesus Would Not Have Taught from the Torah If It Was Corrupted

If Jesus knew that the Torah was corrupted, he would not have used it to teach. Yet the Gospels are filled with examples of Jesus not only quoting and confirming verses and prophecies from the Torah, but also reading directly from it. In Luke 4:16-21, Jesus:

> came to Nazareth, where He had been brought up. And as His custom was, He went into the synagogue on the Sabbath day, and stood up to read and the scroll of the prophet Isaiah was handed to him. Unrolling it, he found the place where it is written: "the spirit of the Lord is upon me, because he has anointed me to preach the Gospel to the poor; he has sent me to heal the brokenhearted, to proclaim liberty to the captives and recovery of sight to the blind, to set at liberty those who are oppressed; to proclaim the acceptable year of the lord."

---

[41] *See* < https://en.wikipedia.org/wiki/Dead_Sea_Scrolls>.

C. If the Torah Were Corrupted, It Would Have Been a Scandal Denounced by Earlier Prophets

1. Overview

If the Torah were corrupted, it would have been a scandal that earlier prophets would have exposed and denounced. Yet none of the works of any of the Old Testament prophets, including Moses, Ezra, David, Solomon, Isaiah, Jeremiah, Ezekiel, Daniel, Hosea, Joel, Amos, Obadiah, Micah, Nahum, Habakkuk, Zephaniah, Haggai, Zechariah, and Malachi, indicate any hint of corruption. There are 61 prophets in Christianity and 66 books in the Bible, and yet none of these make any mention of the corruption of the Scripture. It seems that if God really did cause his truth to be revealed to these prophets, then the first thing He would have told them to speak is to not trust the Scriptures that had been handed down to them, as these had been corrupted by men. Yet there is not a single reference to such corruption in all of the books in the Bible.

2. Jesus Reaffirmed and Confirmed the Old Testament

Jesus reaffirms and confirms the books of the Old Testament, stating (Mat 5:17-18):

> Do not think that I came to destroy the Law or the Prophets. I did not come to destroy but to fulfill. For assuredly, I say to you, till heaven and earth pass away, one jot or one tittle will by no means pass from the law till all is fulfilled.

In Luke 4, Jesus came to Nazareth, went into the synagogue on the Sabbath day, and stood up to read the scroll of the prophet Isaiah. He read (Luke 4:18-19):

> the spirit of the Lord is upon me, because he has anointed me to preach the Gospel to the poor; he has sent me to heal the brokenhearted, to proclaim liberty to the captives and recovery of sight to the blind, to set at liberty those who are oppressed; to proclaim the acceptable year of the lord."

Jesus then closed the book, sat down, and (Luke 4:21):

> He began to say to them, "Today this Scripture is fulfilled in your hearing."

Had Jesus been reading from corrupted words, surely he would not have stated that the Scripture that he had just read had been fulfilled. Rather, he would have stated that he just read a corrupted text but that he was going to fulfill another text, one that unscrupulous men had successfully obliterated and left no trace of.

3. The Scripture Teaches that It is Profitable for Doctrine and Instruction, Not that It Has Been Corrupted

If the Scriptures had been corrupted, then surely Paul, who wrote 2 Timothy and was a master of the Hebrew Scriptures, would have known about it and would have exposed the corruption. Instead, Paul affirms the place of Scripture and its value for doctrine, teaching, and instruction. In 2 Timothy, Paul writes:

> 2Ti 3:15 and that from childhood you have known the Holy Scriptures, which are able to make you wise for salvation through faith which is in Christ Jesus.

> 2Ti 3:16 All Scripture is given by inspiration of God, and is profitable for doctrine, for reproof, for correction, for instruction in righteousness,

> 2Ti 3:17 that the man of God may be complete, thoroughly equipped for every good work.

Revelation also affirms that God will punish anyone who adds to His prophecy or removes words from His book (Rev 22:18-19):

> For I testify to everyone who hears the words of the prophecy of this book: If anyone adds to these things, God will add to him the plagues that are written in this book;

> and if anyone takes away from the words of the book of this prophecy, God shall take away his part from the Book of Life, from the holy city, and from the things which are written in this book.

D. If the Scriptures Were Corrupted, It Would Mean that *Allāh* was Impotent against the Greatest Cover-Up in History

If Islam were true, then it would mean that over the past 5,000 years, corrupted men managed to completely obliterate any trace of *Allāh's* original message. That is a remarkable feat. More than this, it means nothing is safe. If man can corrupt the message of 61 prophets and 66 books of the Bible, how can we ensure that he cannot corrupt the *Qur'ān*? Moreover, how do we know that the *Qur'ān* as we have it today was not already corrupted? What is to stop unscrupulous men from destroying every *Qur'ān* manuscript since the seventh century and ever *ḥadīth* ever written and change them all to state that, in fact, it was neither Isaac nor Ishmael that was the son of promise, but rather, it was Midian, the fourth son of Abraham by Keturah? Indeed, the Islamic narrative casts a great deal of doubt on the reliability of any holy text.

Muslims respond to this challenge by arguing that Muhammad was the seal of the Prophets and therefore, the Qur'ān could not have been corrupted. *'Āyah* 33:40 states:

> Muhammad is not the father of any of your men, but he is the Messenger of Allah and the Seal of the prophets And Allah is ever Knower of all things.

Muslims also point to *'Āyah* 15:9 as evidence that the *Qur'ān* has been preserved:

> Surely We have revealed the Reminder, and surely We are its Guardian.

إِنَّا نَحْنُ نَزَّلْنَا الذِّكْرَ وَإِنَّا لَهُ لَحَافِظُونَ.

The problem with this argument is that by relying on this verse, it assumes that it has not already been corrupted. If unscrupulous men were able to change and corrupt all of the manuscripts of the 66 books of the Bible and all of the messages of the 61 prophets of the Bible without leaving a trace, then surely they could have changed all of the manuscripts of the *Qur'ān* without a trace and then changed the message of *'Āyah* 33:40 and *'Āyah* 15:9 to state that *Allāh* has preserved the *Qur'ān*.

Chapter 8. Valid Points

A. Points that are True, but Insignificant

1. Jehoiachin's Age When He Became King

a) Claim:

Dr. Philips writes (p. 24):

> In 2nd Chronicles, Jehoiachin was described as being eight years old when he began to reign, while in 2nd Kings he is described as being eighteen years old.

The NKJV translates 2 Kings 24:8 and 2 Chronicles 36:9 as follows:

> 2Ki 24:8 Jehoiachin was <u>eighteen</u> years old when he became king, and he reigned in Jerusalem three months.

> 2Ch 36:9 Jehoiachin was <u>eight</u> years old when he became king, and he reigned in Jerusalem three months and ten days.

b) Response: The Contradiction Is Evidence of Scribal Errors in Early Manuscripts

At 2 Chronicles 36:9, the NIV Bible states that Jehoiachin was 18 years old when he became King. The verse contains the following note at "n":

> One Hebrew manuscript; some Septuagint manuscripts and Syriac (see also 2 Kings 24:8); most Hebrew manuscripts *eight*

The NIV Bible thus reconciles the contradiction between 2 Kings 24:8 and 2 Chronicles 36:9 by adopting the age given in one Hebrew manuscript (18 years of age), even though most Hebrew manuscripts state that Jehoiachin was 8 years old when he became king.

We can conclude that the most likely cause of the contradiction between 2 Kings 24:8 and 2 Chronicles 24:8 in the ASV, FLS, ISV,

KJV, LBLA, MKJV, NKJV, RSV, SRV, SSE and SVD is not a contradiction in the original manuscript of 2 Kings and 2 Chronicles, but rather, with respect to the transmission of the original texts over thousands of years through scribal errors. Most Hebrew manuscripts copied "8," but one Hebrew manuscript, some Septuagint manuscripts and Syriac copied down "18" in 2 Chronicles 36:9. Since 2 Kings 24:8 mentions "18," the Hebrew, Septuagint and Syriac manuscripts that copied "18" are probably the correct ones.

What this shows is not necessarily that there is a contradiction in the books of the Bible proper, but rather, that in the thousands of years of copying the Hebrew manuscripts, discrepancies emerged in how scribes and translators passed down the texts. It may never be possible to recover the original manuscript of 2 Chronicles 36:9 that stated Jehoiachin's true age, but it would be reasonable to conclude that the original stated that he was 18 years old, in accordance with 2 Kings 24:8.

Therefore, while Dr. Philips is correct in pointing out that there is an inconsistency between the text of 2 Kings 24:8 and the text of 2 Chronicles 36:9 in many translations of the Bible, this cannot be characterized as evidence of the unreliability of the Bible's original texts; rather, it is to be attributed to the choices that translators made when choosing between which ancient manuscripts to rely upon when preparing their translations.

2.   The Manuscripts on Which the Bible is Based are Discrepant

a)   Claim

Dr. Philips quotes from the Preface of *The Holy Bible: Revised Standard Version* to argue that the Bible is unreliable. He reproduces the following passages from the Preface (p. 11-12):

> … the King James Version has grave defects. By the middle of the nineteenth century, the development of Biblical studies and the discovery of many manuscripts more ancient than those upon which the King James Version was based, made it manifest that these defects are so many and so serious as to call for revision of the English translation …

The King James Version of the New Testament was based upon a Greek text that was marred by mistakes, containing the accumulated errors of fourteen centuries of manuscript copying …

b) Response: The Discrepancies to which Dr. Philips Refers Are Immaterial to the Gospel Message

(1) Discrepancies between Manuscripts Are Not Material

It is true that scholars have found some minor discrepancies between the manuscripts that have been used to prepare translations of the Bible. But what are these discrepancies? Do they alter the overall message of the Scriptures? Dr. Bilal Philips provides the following example (p. 13):

> In the Revised Standard Version of the Bible, a number of key verses from the King James Version of the Old and the New Testaments, which Biblical scholars concluded were added in later centuries, were removed from the text and placed in the footnotes. For example, the famous passage in the Gospel of John 8.7 about an adulteress who was about to be stoned. Jesus was supposed to have said: 'Let him who is without sin among you be the first to throw a stone at her' The footnotes of the Revised Standard Version of the Bible (1952) state 'The most ancient authorities omit 7.53-8.11.'

The NIV Study Bible states in brackets: "The earliest manuscripts and many other ancient witnesses do not have John 7:53 – 8:11" (p. 1611). The footnote states:

> This story may not have belonged originally to the Gospel of John. It is absent from almost all the important early manuscripts and those that have it sometimes place it elsewhere (*e.g.*, after Luke 21:28). But the story may well be authentic.

The example that Dr. Philips provides, even if it is based on true information, does not in any way alter the overall meaning and message of the Scriptures—that God so loved the world that he gave his one and only Son, so that everyone who believes in him will have eternal life (John 3:16).

(2) Other Two-Thousand-Year-Old Manuscripts Would be Subject to Similar Discrepancies

One must bear in mind that the Bible is nearly 2,000 years old. It is natural that some discrepancies would enter the manuscripts over the centuries. This is a natural result of human error and does not in any way conclusively prove that intent of scribes to change the message of the early apostles, as suggested by Dr. Philips.

3. The Authors of Many of the Old Testament Books of the Bible Are Unknown

a) Argument

Dr. Philips writes (p. 17-18):

> In the appendix of the Revised Standard Version entitled "Books of the Bible," the following is written concerning the authorship of over one third of the remaining books of the Old Testament:

Books	Authors
Judges	Possibly Samuel
Ruth	Perhaps Samuel
First Samuel	Unknown
Second Samuel	Unknown
First Kings	Unknown
Second Kings	Unknown
First Chronicles	Unknown
Esther	Unknown
Job	Unknown
Ecclesiastes	Doubtful
Jonah	Unknown
Malachi	Nothing known

Dr. Philips does not explain the relevance of this excerpt from the RSV. Presumably, what he is suggesting is that because the authors of so many books of the Old Testament are, according to the editors of the RSV, unknown, the texts themselves cannot be trusted.

b) Response

There are several problems with the suggested view:

- Just because we do not know who wrote a text does not mean it cannot be divinely inspired. What we know is that Moses wrote some or all of the Pentateuch. Other authors may have contributed to the writing or to the compilation. This does not invalidate their divine inspiration. Similarly, some of the writers of other books of the Old Testament, such as First and Second Samuel and First and Second Kings, are unconfirmed. Tradition suggests that Jeremiah wrote First and Second Kings, but scholars believe these books were written by various authors. To suggest that these texts are invalid or unreliable because they were not written by Jeremiah would be to state that the *Qur'ān* is unreliable because it was not written by Muhammad; rather, it was, according to Islamic tradition, recited by Muhammad and transcribed by scribes.
- Oral tradition played an important role in passing down and preserving the texts in the Old and New Testaments. Stories were told by generations and then passed down and written down. This is not unlike the Islamic tradition whereby scribes wrote down the words recited by Prophet Muhammad. To state that a religious text could only be valid if written by a prophet would be to invalidate the *Qur'ān* in its entirety.

4. Moses Could Not Have Authored the Entirety of the Pentateuch

a) Argument

Dr. Philips writes (p. 14):

The first five books of the Bible (the Pentateuch) are traditionally attributed to Prophet Moses, however, there are many verses within these books which indicate that Prophet Moses could not possibly have written everything in them. For example, Deuteronomy 34.5-8 states: "5 So Moses the servant of the Lord died there in the land of Moab, according to the word of the Lord, 6 and he buried him in the valley of the land of Moab opposite Beth-peor but no man knows the place of his burial to this day 7 Moses was a hundred and twenty years old when he died his eye was not dim, nor his natural force abated 8 And the people of Israel wept for Moses in the plains of Moab thirty days then the days of weeping and mourning for Moses ended " It is quite obvious that someone else wrote these verses about Prophet Moses' death.

Deuteronomy 34:5-8 states as follows:

> Deu 34:5 So Moses the servant of the LORD died there in the land of Moab, according to the word of the LORD.

> Deu 34:6 And He buried him in a valley in the land of Moab, opposite Beth Peor; but no one knows his grave to this day.

> Deu 34:7 Moses was one hundred and twenty years old when he died. His eyes were not dim nor his natural vigor diminished.

> Deu 34:8 And the children of Israel wept for Moses in the plains of Moab thirty days. So the days of weeping and mourning for Moses ended.

It is not possible that Moses wrote these verses because he would have already been dead at the time they were written.

b) Reply

(1) Moses Could Have Written the Entirety of the Pentateuch

It is entirely possible that Moses penned the entirety of the Pentateuch, including events he did not witness. God, who gave Moses supernatural revelation about what happened at the beginning of the Creation of the Universe, which Moses did not witness, could have also supernaturally revealed to Moses what would happen after Moses's death. In fact, God revealed to Moses several future events that Moses did not personally witness, including:

- Israel's future earthly kings (Genesis 36:31; Deuteronomy 17:14-15);
- The coming of Jesus (Genesis 3:15, 12:1-3, 22:18, 49:10, Numbers 24:17; Deuteronomy 18:15-18).

If Moses was divinely inspired about events that would happen hundreds of years after his death, he could also write about his own death.

(2) Another Author's Contribution to the Pentateuch Would Not Undermine the Validity of the Texts

It is also possible that although Moses wrote the Pentateuch, the last few sentences in Deuteronomy could have been written by another inspired writer, such as Joshua. This does not necessarily undermine the validity of the Pentateuch books, which merely state that Moses wrote the books, not that "only" Moses wrote the books and that no other author contributed thereto. Therefore, it is possible that the account of the death of Moses could have been authored by a later writer, without undermining the validity or historicity of the texts or of Moses's contribution to the texts.

5. Discrepancies in Manuscripts Recounting Jesus' Genealogy in Luke 3:33

a) Overview

Dr. Philips writes that Matthew's and Luke's lists (p. 27-28):

> meet again at Abraham and between David and Abraham most of the names are the same. However, in Matthew's list, Hezron's son's name is Ram, the father of Ammin'adab, while in Luke's list, Hezron's son's name is Arni whose son's name is Admin, the father of Ammin'adab. Consequently, between David and Abraham there are 12 forefathers in Matthew's list and 13 in Luke's list.

The discrepancies noted by Dr. Philips arise in certain translations of the Bible. Matthew's account is consistent across mainstream translations; the NKJV, NIV, ASV, and RSV provide an account of Hezron, who begot Ram, who begot Amminadab. However, some translations of Luke, such as the ASV and RSV, state that Arni rather than Ram was the son of Hezron, while other translations, such as the NIV and NKJV, state that Ram was the son of Hezron. This appears to be due to discrepancies in the original manuscripts.

b) Matthew Genealogy: Identical Across Translations

The passages in Matthew are identical across mainstream translations, including the NKJV, NIV, ASV, and RSV, as follows:
- Abraham
- Isaac
- Jacob
- Judah
- Perez
- Hezron
- Ram
- Amminadab
- Nahshon

- Salmon
- Boaz
- Obed
- Jesse
- David

c) Luke Genealogy: Discrepancies in Some Translations

(1) Overview

There are discrepancies in the translations of Luke, as follows:

Luke	NIV, NKJV	ASV, BBE	RSV
3:34	Abraham	Abraham	Abraham
	Isaac	Isaac	Isaac
	Jacob	Jacob	Jacob
3:33	Judah	Judah	Judah
	Perez	Perez	Perez
	Hezron	Hezron	Hezron
	Ram	***Arni***	***Arni***
			Admin
	Amminadab	Amminadab	Amminadab
3:32	Nahshon	Nahshon	Nahshon
	Salmon	Salmon	***Sala***
	Boaz	Boaz	Boaz
	Obed	Obed	Obed
	Jesse	Jesse	Jesse
3:31	David	David	David

The NIV Study Bible states in note "n" at Luke 3:33 the following:

> Some manuscripts *Amminadab, the son of Admin, the son of Arni*; other manuscripts vary widely.

This thus appears to be a genuine transcript issue in the transmission of early manuscripts.

(2) Response

While Dr. Philips is correct in pointing out that there are some discrepancies in the genealogy recounted in Luke, the discrepancies are so minor as to have no practical effect as to the overall history recounted. It makes no difference whether the name of Hezron's descendent was Ram, as recounted in the NIV and NKJV, or Arni, as recounted in the ASV, BBE and RSV. The fact that the RSV includes an extra descendent, Admin, between Arni and Amminadab, is not necessarily indicative of a contradiction; it is possible that the RSV relied on a manuscript that included an extra generation that other manuscripts skipped, with the overall line remaining intact. Similarly, whether Nahshon's descendent was named Salmon, as recounted in the NIV, NKJV, ASV and BBE, or Sala, as recounted in the RSV, is of no import. It is possible that Sala was an alternative name or a nickname for Salmon. Regardless, all of the translations confirm the same line between Abraham and David, and whether the name of one of the lines in the generation was Salmon or Sala does not affect this overall message.

B. Point that is True and Significant: Omission of the 1 John 5:7 Account of the Trinity from the American Standard Version (1901) and Revised Standard Version (1952)

1. Overview

Dr. Philips writes (p. 14):

> In 1 John 5.7, Jesus was supposed to have said: "There are three that bear record in heaven, the Father, the Word, and the Holy Ghost and these three are one."18 The well-known Biblical scholar, Benjamin Wilson, writes that this text concerning the "heavenly witness" is not contained in any Greek manuscript which was written earlier than the 15th century! Consequently, in the Revised Standard Version, this verse was deleted from the text without even so much as a footnote. However, in order to keep the total number of verses in the Revised Standard Version the same as that of the King James Version, the revisers split verse 6 into two verses.

It is true that whereas the KJV (1611) contained the entirety of "This is he that came by water and blood, even Jesus Christ; not by water only, but by water and blood. And it is the Spirit that beareth witness, because the Spirit is truth" as 1 John 5:6, the ASV (1901) and RSV (1952), which was based on the ASV, have split 1 John 5:6 into two verses, 1 John 5:6 and 1 John 5:7, and have omitted the text of 1 John 5:7 ("For there are three that bear witness in heaven: the Father, the Word, and the Holy Spirit; and these three are one") entirely.

The following table breaks down the way the KJV, on the one hand, and the ASV and RSV, on the other, label 1 John 5:6 and 1 John 5:8, and how the ASV and RSV omit the text of 1 John 5:7 that is found in the KJV.

Verse	KJV	ASV	RSV	NIV
This is he that came by water and blood, Jesus Christ. Not only by water, but by water and blood.	1Jn 5:6	1Jn 5:6	1Jn 5:6	1Jn 5:6
It is the Spirit who bears witness, because the Spirit is truth.		1Jn 5:7	1Jn 5:7	
For there are three that bear record in heaven, the Father, the Word, and the Holy Ghost: and these three are one.	1Jn 5:7	NA	NA	NA
There are three that bear witness [in earth]	1Jn 5:8	1Jn 5:8	1Jn 5:8	1Jn 5:7
The Spirit, and the water, and the blood; these three agree in one				1Jn 5:8

The KJV states:

1Jn 5:6 This is he that came by water and blood, even Jesus Christ; not by water only, but by water and blood. And it is the Spirit that beareth witness, because the Spirit is truth.

1Jn 5:7 For there are three that bear record in heaven, the Father, the Word, and the Holy Ghost: and these three are one.

1Jn 5:8 And there are three that bear witness in earth, the Spirit, and the water, and the blood: and these three agree in one.

The ASV states:

1Jn 5:6 This is he that came by water and blood, even Jesus Christ; not with the water only, but with the water and with the blood.

1Jn 5:7 And it is the Spirit that beareth witness, because the Spirit is the truth.

1Jn 5:8 For there are three who bear witness, the Spirit, and the water, and the blood: and the three agree in one.

2.   Response

The footnote to 1 John 5:7 in the *NIV Study Bible* states:

> At the end of this verse, some older English versions add the words found in the NIV text note. But the addition is not found in any Greek manuscript or NT translation prior to the 16th century.

The NIV text note for verses 7 and 8 states:

> Late manuscripts of the Vulgate: *testify in heaven: the Father, the Word and the Holy Spirit, and these three are one. And there are three that testify on earth: the* (not found in any Greek manuscript before the sixteenth century)

Accordingly, the NIV, along with other translation including the ASV and RSV, eliminated the text in verse 5:7 of the KJV and reassigned verse 5:7 to the text immediately preceding it (as in the case of the ASV and RSV) or the text immediately following it (as with the NIV).

On this basis, we can conclude that there is, in fact, a discrepancy between the English translations of 1 John 5. However, if we base the translations on the original Greek manuscripts, we can conclude that the text in verse 5:7 of the KJV did not exist in John's original letter.

This does not, however, impugn the divine inspiration of the Bible. It impugns only the validity of certain translations of the Bible that added a verse not contained in the original Greek manuscripts. This reaffirms a truth that the Bible teaches—man is imperfect, fallible and flawed. Only God is perfect.

The problem with 1 John 5:7 is not fatal to the overall message and reliability of the Bible. In fact, scholars recognize that mistakes have been made in both transcribing and translating the original manuscripts of the Bible. However, they recognize that such errors are almost always harmless and, where variations are substantial, they represent a minute portion of the entire text.

For example, Brooke Foss Westcott and Fenton John Anthony Hort, the editors of *The New Testament in the Original Greek*, an 1881 Greek version of the New Testament upon which the ASV and RSV were based, found that without orthographic differences, doubtful textual variants exist in only one sixtieth of the entire New Testament, with most of them being comparatively trivial variations, and that substantial variations form hardly more than one thousandth of the entire text.[42] *The New Testament in the Original Greek* is a critical text compiled from some of the oldest New Testament fragments and texts that had been discovered at the time. Westcott and Hort concluded that there were no signs of deliberate falsification of the text for dogmatic purposes.

---

[42] Brooke Foss Westcott and Fenton John Anthony Hort, *The New Testament in the original Greek*, Vol. 2, Introduction and Appendix (London: Macmillan, 1896), p. 2.

Chapter 9. Conclusion

A careful study of the Christian scriptures demonstrates serious weaknesses in Dr. Philips' arguments. The use of sources employed by Dr. Philips to challenge Christianity is problematic in that he cites sources that very often cannot be found or verified. Where sources can be verified, the use of sources proves only that there are scholars who challenge the reliability of the Bible, not that the Bible is in fact unreliable.

The various claims that Dr. Philips makes are flawed and refutable. These claims include, but are not limited to, the following:

- The authors of the Gospels are unknown;
- The Bible contradicts itself;
- The early church opposed iconography because it was a form of idolatry;
- Isaiah 42 prophesies the coming of Muhammad; and
- Muhammad was the promised "comforter" (*paraklētos*) prophesied in John 14:16.

As demonstrated in this book, Dr. Philips' claims are not historically grounded and often misrepresent history and misconstrue the text and meanings of the Bible.

In addition, Dr. Philips argues Jesus upheld Jewish ceremonial laws, which Islam continues to uphold, but Paul changed Jesus' message by abolishing Old Testament rules, including laws on circumcision, ritual slaughter, ablution before prayer, prostration in prayer, veiling, tithing, fasting, polygamy and prohibitions on pork, alcohol and levying interest. However, a careful study of the Bible demonstrates that Dr. Philips has distorted the Mosaic law, trying to make it appear to coincide with current Islamic law and obscuring the very stark and important differences between the Mosaic law and Islamic law. A careful examination also reveals that Dr. Philips fails to recognize that Jesus fulfilled the Mosaic law through his sacrifice on the cross. In teaching that Christians were no longer under the Mosaic law, Paul was reaffirming the message of the cross.

Dr. Philips often employs circular reasoning to support his claims. For example, in defending his claim that Jesus is not God, Dr. Philips attacks verses where Jesus states that He is the Lord by arguing that Jesus could not have been the speaker because the speaker says that He is the Lord. This is the case, for example, in Revelation 1:8, where Dr. Philips assumes that Jesus could not be the speaker because the verse states that the "Lord" is the speaker. In other words, Jesus is not the Lord and the biblical verses that state otherwise are mistaken and corrupted because Jesus is not the Lord. Such reasoning is preposterously circular. Moreover, Dr. Philips ignores the very clear context in the three verses preceding and following Revelation 1:8, which make it clear that the speaker is Jesus. This betrays a tactic whereby Dr. Philips first decides what he wishes to argue and then attacks the verses that demonstrate the opposite of what he wants to argue by denying the clear and patent message conveyed by those verses, or denying that the verses were ever accurately passed down to us to begin with.

Moreover, Dr. Philips' claims with respect to the corruption of the Bible, including the Torah in particular and the Old Testament in general, are flawed. First, the *Qur'ān* teaches in *'Āyah* 61:6 that Jesus confirmed the Torah. If that is the case, then Muslims should read and believe the Torah. Second, if the Torah were corrupted in Jesus' time, then Jesus would not have taught from it. Yet the Gospels are filled with many examples of Jesus quoting and confirming verses and prophecies from the Torah, as when He read from the book of Isaiah at the synagogue in Nazareth (Luke 4:16-21) and stated that not "one jot or one tittle" will "pass from the law till all is fulfilled" (Mat 5:18). Third, if the Torah were corrupted, then Jesus or earlier prophets would have exposed and denounced such corruption. Yet none of the works of any of the prophets make mention of any corruption. Finally, if the Bible were corrupted, as Dr. Philips claims, then it would signify one of the greatest scandals and cover-ups in human history, and one that *Allāh* was evidently impotent to stop.

Some of Dr. Philips' claims about the Bible are correct, though ultimately they relate to minor or ancillary points that do not support his overall message about the unreliability of the Bible. For example, he points out that in 2 Chronicles, Jehoiachin is said to have been eight years old when he began to reign, while in 2 Kings, he is said to have been eighteen years old. Similarly, Dr. Philips states that scholars have found some discrepancies between the manuscripts that have been used to prepare translations of the Bible. He cites a footnote in the Revised Standard Version of the Bible that states that the most ancient authorities omit John 7:53-8:11, which recounts the story of the adulteress who was caught in adultery and brought before Jesus, who said, "Let him who is without sin among you be the first to throw a stone at her" (John 8:7).

Dr. Philips is not mistaken in his assertions. However, the points that he raises are generally insignificant and do not alter the overall message of the Bible. For example, whether the passage of the adulteress caught in adultery in John 7:53-8:11 is included in the earliest authorities does not detract from the Bible's central message. That is a message of forgiveness and God's reconciliation with man through the sacrifice of His Son, Jesus Christ: "For God so loved the world that he gave His one and only Son, so that everyone who believes in him will have eternal life" (John 3:16). Moreover, the central message of John 7:53-8:11—that we should look at our own sins before accusing our neighbor of sinning—is repeated elsewhere throughout the Scriptures. For example, in Matthew 7:5, Jesus teaches us that before we "remove the speck from your brother's eye," we should first "remove the plank" from your own eyes.

In addition, Dr. Philips writes that the authors of many of the books of the Bible are unknown. While scholars do not unanimously agree on who authored some of the books of the Bible, this does not mean that the books are unreliable. Just because the author of a text is unknown does not mean the text cannot be divinely inspired, nor does it mean that the text could not have been inspired by a divinely-inspired prophet and then put into written form by an unknown scribe. Moreover, just because some scholars contend that more than one writer contributed to the Pentateuch does not mean that Moses did not also contribute to some or most of it.

Dr. Philips also points to the discrepancies in manuscripts recounting Jesus' genealogy in Luke 3:33. For example, Nahshon's descendent was named Salmon according to the NIV, NKJV, ASV and BBE, but his name was Sala according to the RSV. However, Sala could have been a nickname for Salmon and, in any case, all of the translations confirm the same line between Abraham and David, regardless of whether the name of one of the lines in the generation was Salmon or Sala.

In the entirety of his book, Dr. Philips does make one point that is both true and significant. On page 14, he writes that

> In 1 John 5.7, Jesus was supposed to have said: "There are three that bear record in heaven, the Father, the Word, and the Holy Ghost and these three are one."18 The well-known Biblical scholar, Benjamin Wilson, writes that this text concerning the "heavenly witness" is not contained in any Greek manuscript which was written earlier than the 15th century! Consequently, in the Revised Standard Version, this verse was deleted from the text without even so much as a footnote. However, in order to keep the total number of verses in the Revised Standard Version the same as that of the King James Version, the revisers split verse 6 into two verses.

It is true that 1 John 5:7 in the KJV ("For there are three that bear record in heaven, the Father, the Word, and the Holy Ghost: and these three are one") is absent from other translations of the Bible, including the ASV, RSV and NIV. This does not, however, impugn the divine inspiration of the Bible; it impugns only the validity of the KJV translation of the Bible, which added a verse not contained in the original Greek manuscripts. This reaffirms a truth that the Bible teaches—man is imperfect, fallible and flawed. Only God is perfect.

Ultimately Dr. Philip's book fails to persuasively demonstrate that man has corrupted the Bible, that the *Qur'ān* is God's true and divinely inspired book and that Jesus' true message is that he is merely a prophet of *Allāh*, as stated in the *Qur'ān*, not the sacrificial lamb that was offered up by God for the salvation of the world, as taught in the Bible. Ultimately, Dr. Philips' book fails to take away the hope that Jesus Christ has given to all who put their faith in Him.

www.ingramcontent.com/pod-product-compliance
Lightning Source LLC
Chambersburg PA
CBHW031621040426
42452CB00007B/608